Walks & Rambles in

DUTCHESS AND PUTNAM COUNTIES

A Guide to Ecology and History in Eastern Hudson Valley Parks

PEGGY TURCO

Photographs by the author

A Walks & Rambles™ Guide

Backcountry Publications
The Countryman Press, Inc.
Woodstock, Vermont

An Invitation to the Reader

Over time trails can be rerouted and signs and landmarks altered. If you find that changes have occurred along the walks described in this book, please let us know so that corrections may be made in future editions. The author and publisher also welcome other comments and suggestions. Address all correspondence to:

Editor
Walks and Rambles™ Series
Backcountry Publications
P.O. Box 175
Woodstock, VT 05091

Library of Congress Cataloging-in-Publication Data

Turco, Peggy.
    Walks & rambles in Dutchess and Putnam Counties : a guide to
ecology and history in Eastern Hudson Valley parks / Peggy Turco.
        p.   cm.
    Includes bibliographical references.
    ISBN 0-88150-169-7
    1. Dutchess County (N.Y.)—Description and travel—Guide-books.
2. Putnam County (N.Y.)—Description and travel—Guide-books
3. Walking—New York (State)—Dutchess County—Guide-books.
4. Walking—New York (State)—Putnam County—Guide-books.
5. Historic sites—New York (State)—Dutchess County—Guide-books.
6. Historic sites—New York (State)—Putnam County—Guide-books.
7. Ecology—New York (State)—Dutchess County—Guide-books.
8. Ecology—New York (State)—Putnam County—Guide-books.
    I. Title.
    F127.D8T87   1990
    917.47'30443—dc20   89-28231
                                                                                        CIP

Published by Backcountry Publications
A division of The Countryman Press, Inc.
Woodstock, Vermont 05091

Printed in the United States of America
Typesetting by NK Graphics
Design by Ann Aspell
Maps and calligraphy by Alex Wallach
Illustrations on pages 18, 70, 164 by He Who Stands Firm
Cover photograph and photograph on page 117 © by Esther Kiviat, 1990

This book is dedicated to the volunteers who design, construct, and maintain the footpaths in our parks and the scientists and naturalists whose research increases our knowledge of our ecosystems.

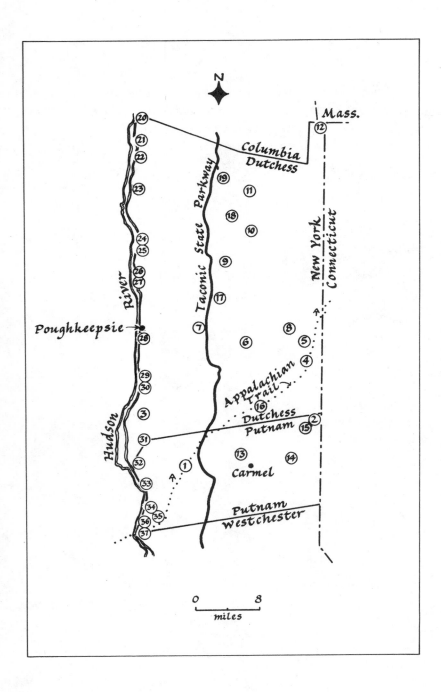

Table of Contents

Acknowledgments

Many people helped with this book. I want to thank all those I met in offices and in the woods and spoke with by phone. Especially I want to thank Roger Cohn, Ray Armater, Melodye Moore, and Tim Countryman for the guided tours of their parks and their gracious help; Kathy Rosborough for all her help on Clermont, particularly her original map that became the map of Clermont in this book; Erik Kiviat of Bard College and Hudsonia for the use of his field notes and his numerous knowledgeable comments; David Oestreicher for his extensive help on Lenape linguistics and history; He Who Stands Firm for his line drawings drawn from life and for accompanying me on many shared walks; John Fuchs and Christina DiMarco of Clove Creek Artists for the use of their darkroom for hours upon hours; Andy Labruzzo, environmental planner for Putnam County, for the chapter on Merritt Park; the kind librarians of Dover Library who helped answer every question with a smile; Esther Kiviat for the use of her glorious photograph of Tivoli Bays; Jim Horend for the chapter on Manitoga; Jim Gackstatter for first showing me Hoyt House and the old trees of Norrie State Park; Helen Lazarides for making Sharparoon available once again to the public and for her help; the Union Vale park board for making Tymor Park available to the public; Kathy Jancek for the tour of Constitution Island; Daisy Suckley for the tea and for the tour of Wilderstein; Rich Parisio and Susan Ashworth for their help on questions concerning Stony Kill; Pam Marshall, Dover recreation director, for her help on Boyce Park; Holly Thomas of the Dutchess County Planning Department for her help on the Harlem Valley Rail-Trail and other parks; Bob Herberger of New York State's Department of Environmental Conservation (DEC) for his help on the multiple use areas; Ken Letters of the DEC for his information on Osborn Preserve; the Putnam County Historical Society for all its help tracing many different pieces of information; the Dutchess County Historical Society; the Fishkill Historical Society; the Nature Conservancy and Greg Seamon; Clearwater for its information on critical habitats of the Hudson River; Garret Storm for his information on the Beacons; Jim Rod for his help with Constitution Marsh; Lee Eaton, Beekman town historian, for her help on history of Depot Hill and The Clove; Homer Staley for the information on Ferncliff; Barry Didato for his information on the Greenway; Lester Collins for his information on Innisfree; Cynthia Grant for the tour of Montgomery Place; James Utter for his help with Pawling Preserve; Mike Malone for his information on Reese Sanctuary; and Glenn Dochtermann for all his help. To all of you, thank you.

Introduction

At one time, Dutchess and Putnam counties were one, but perhaps because their land forms suggest a natural separation along the old patent lines, this region on the eastern shore of the Hudson River was split into two counties in 1812. Putnam County, to the south, is all hills: the cordillera of the Appalachian Mountains, the ridges like fish backs running southwest to northeast. Dutchess County, to the north, contains north-south tending Appalachian ridges, some quite high, but there are also broad, flat valleys, lowlands, even plains. Putnam County is nearly all metamorphic resistant, Hudson Highlands Pre-cambrian granite and gneiss. Dutchess contains schist and sedimentary limestones, sandstones, shales, and slates of various ages.

Both counties lie within the eastern deciduous woodlands biome of North America and contain plant communities that are, to a certain extent, predictable according to soil type. On the slopes one expects to find oak and sugar maple forests; in the swamps grow red maple, ash, and elm; and in the marshes, cattail and phragmites. Hemlock grows in cool ravines and on sheltered moist flats, north-facing slopes, and ridge-top pockets. These flora associations are characteristic of the region, as is the degree of agricultural abandonment, industrial and housing development, and pollution. Dutchess and Putnam counties are an ecological and economic continuum along a north-to-south gradient of climate, species, and human population change.

It is the Hudson River—not actually a river here but a tidal estuary—which sets these two counties apart as special among eastern woodlands. The region is rich in flora and fauna as well as recreational, industrial, historical, and aesthetic resources. Putnam County contains practically *all* of the world-famous Hudson Highlands east of the river. Dutchess County contains almost *all* of Millionaire's Row, the estates of America's early industrialists.

There is much to explore in Dutchess and Putnam counties and much to learn about the ecology of the Hudson River. This book is a short guide to the ecology and history of parks where the public has legal and simple access. The novice naturalist and walker can use this book as the beginning to greater understanding of our area. Seasoned hikers may use this guide to explore places with which they are unfamiliar.

This guide is divided into four sections: The forested Inland Hills; the section on New York State Multiple Use Areas; Millionaires' Row along the Hudson River in Dutchess County; and the Hudson Highlands along the Hudson River in Putnam County.

If you are unfamiliar with terrestrial succession, you may wish to start with the Pawling Preserve chapter, which explains why different trees live in different places. This will give you a grounding in ecological thought. The rest of the chapters expand on different seasonal, ecological, and historical topics, and accommodate a wide range of hiking ability, from short walks for beginners to full-day mountain hikes and bushwhacks.

Below are a few things to keep in mind when you are walking.

INDIAN PLACE NAMES

Many place names in Putnam and Dutchess counties are said to be Lenape or Mahican words. The Lenape or Delaware people are classified into two basic linguistic groups: Unami and Munsee. Munsee was spoken on both banks of the lower and mid-Hudson and upper Delaware River Valleys, while Unami was spoken south of the Raritan River and the Delaware Water Gap. Mahicans, a closely related people, lived throughout the lower and middle Hudson Valley north into the Champlain Valley.

Although scholars have been studying Lenape and Mahican names for decades, a great deal of controversy still exists over their origin and meaning, especially since the Mahican language is extinct. It is only recently that the Lenape people have been consulted as to the meaning of Lenape names. Many of the place names are archaic words that come from dialects that are no longer spoken, and practically all have been corrupted by non-native people who, unfamiliar with Native languages, had no idea how to write the sounds they thought they heard. The words have become almost unrecognizable. David Oestreicher, a Lenape scholar and linguist, offers one example. Outside New York City is the place name "Rockaway." At first glance it seems to be a European word, perhaps barely Lenape. But as Oestreicher asked Native speakers about the word and delved into other sources, he found that the word was originally *lechqua acki*, which means "a sandy place." Throughout the text I have attempted to explain, where possible, the meaning and origin of the Native place names.

POISON IVY

The Hudson Valley is famous for its poison ivy (*Rhus radicans*). Nowhere else does the soil, humidity, and temperature combine for such excellent and luxuriant results. Expect it in the parks you walk. Learn the plant. Avoid it. And be glad it grows. Poison ivy berries, white and ripe by fall, are a major food source for over sixty species of birds as well as for deer, black bear, mice, rabbit, muskrat, and fox. It keeps them alive. Can you imagine, *eating poison ivy berries?*

MOSQUITOES

When Swedish naturalist Peter Kalm visited the Hudson Valley in 1749, he wrote in his journal, "I never saw the mosquitoes more plentiful in any part of America than they are here." He was specifically describing the upper Hudson, but we get our fair share here in the mid-Hudson.

Especially in the lowland (but not the highland) parks that border the Hudson River, expect a summer nightmare of mosquitoes when the temperature and rainfall lead to a big hatching. You may want to save those parks for some other time of year.

BUSHWHACKING

Trails buffer the walker from the woods. Though a great convenience, trails prevent a true experience of the habitat they pass. Once you are used to trails and become more experienced in the woods, try bushwhacking now and then.

A bushwhack is the best way to see the woods. For instance, it's one thing to walk through a laurel thicket on a trail, another to bushwhack through it. Bushwhacking through a laurel thicket will open your Native American heart and eyes. You'll know mountain laurel to the core of its being, gain a deeper understanding of its ecology and its relationships with its environment, even though you curse and call the thicket a laurel hell. Bushwhacking will lead you to intimate groves and deep hollows that will be all your own.

Some preserves require that you keep to trails since trails funnel compaction and minimize damage. Many of these parks contain rare or endangered plants and animals. Even a little trampling in the wrong spot can be devastating. At sites where you know the flora is fragile,

The author leading a nature walk at the Vanderbilt Mansion.

such as on top of Brace Mountain or at private preserves such as Manitoga, never bushwhack. But on forested slopes with thicker soils, fields, and in valleys, with care and attention to footwork, the walker can bushwhack occasionally with little harm to the soil and flora. New York State's Multiple Use Areas are prime bushwhack territory. Make it a habit to step between plants, not on them. Duck beneath branches rather than break them. So long as you do not visit the same site regularly, there should be little disturbance to wildlife. If you find yourself near a hawk or owl nest, immediately quit the area.

LYME DISEASE

Lyme disease is a nationwide problem now, and you should be familiar with the symptoms in case by chance you are bitten by a deer tick infected by Lyme disease. Adult and nymph deer ticks are tiny creatures, often no larger than the dot over this "i." Not all deer ticks are infected with the spirochete that causes Lyme disease, so don't panic should you find one attached to your skin. Gently remove it whole and intact, and either send the beast for testing or watch yourself for the temporary red circular skin rash followed by flu-like symptoms of fever, fatigue, nausea, chills, headache, and enlarged lymph nodes. Prompt diagnosis and antibiotic treatment cure the disease. Left to run its course, it can cripple you.

Some people advocate wearing light clothing in the woods, the better to spot a tick on its way up your leg. Also recommended is the tucking of pant legs into socks, so the ticks climb onto your light-colored clothes where they'll get spotted. Various pesticides with high amounts of diethyltoluamine, DEET, are used as tick repellents but only apply such strong poisons to your clothes, never your skin.

FLORA AND FAUNA

Investigating the plants or animals described in this book does not necessitate the picking of a single plant or the taking of a single animal. Such practices are forbidden in most parks and preserves. Bend *down* to look at that flower, do not pick it. Watch that frog from a distance, or *let it come to you*. Teach children who walk with you to respect living things.

FOR THE BEGINNING HIKER

It is easy to be miserable in the woods. The bugs are biting, the poison ivy is thriving, Lyme disease threatens, it's too cold, it's too hot, you're tired; the list of discomforts can be endless. Biting bugs are nasty, it's true, but don't allow them to overwhelm you. Ignore them. Take them in stride. Discomfort is more a thing of the mind. Dwell on mosquitoes and you'll be eaten alive, never again to set foot on a trail. Dwell on the beauty of the trees and the open air and, no matter how much they bite, you'll barely notice the bugs. The more you dwell on a negative thing, the larger it grows. Don't let discomforts ruin your rambles. Don't let fear keep you from the woods.

THE GENTLE ART OF WALKING

Most people walk with their eyes on the trail. This seems only natural, yet how many deer have trail watchers not seen until the animal leaped away? How many flowers in bloom, rare birds, or gorgeous views have they missed? Walking with attention on the ground is unnatural and unexciting.

The woodsperson and rambler looks around at the world, not down at the trail. Develop the artful walk of the observer. Glance ahead several yards and note the condition of the trail. Are there holes, logs, or stones in the path? In that instant, memorize the trail. This leaves you free to walk those yards with your eyes on the woods and your head up, breathing in the wind and glancing in all directions as you go. The world is yours. Use the full range of your vision; see with your peripheral vision not only the center. See all around you at once. Be alert for the movement of animals and the shapes of plants. When the memorized yards are up, glance ahead once more.

At first, this may be hard. It means breaking a habit and overcoming the fear of tripping. Striding along a trail at night in the woods without light is a good way to overcome this fear. With a little practice, this walking technique becomes automatic. Eventually, your feet will know when to swerve to avoid a rock, and you will know when you should glance down to step over a log. Children, especially, quickly develop this skill of the art of walking.

TRAIL CONDITIONS

Trails change, boundaries move, once abundant plants and animals can disappear. There is much "here today, gone tomorrow" in any ecosystem. If you find a change in things as described in this book, write and let me know.

Be prepared and equipped when you enter a park, especially on a full-day hike. In a light pack, take food, water, a trail map, compass, and extra clothes. Carry rain gear if the weather is questionable. Wear sturdy hiking shoes or boots. If you go alone, let someone know where you are heading. It is best—especially for women—not to walk alone in parks near urban areas. Remember that high places such as Brace Mountain, South Beacon Mountain, and Anthony's Nose can be much colder than the surrounding lowlands. A warm spring or autumn day in the valley may become a cold, windy, raw day on the mountaintop. In both these seasons, carry a hat and gloves. Also be aware that the same day's weather in northern Dutchess County can be different from that in Putnam or southern Dutchess counties.

Many people prefer to hike the high hills when the leaves are down, the better to see the views. This is especially true of places like Hell Hollow in the Beacon Range, which is at its best when the cold and the wind make things dramatic. There also aren't any bugs.

On top of Sugarloaf looking downriver to Anthony's Nose and Bear Mountain.

For each park, I have noted the route distance and approximate walking time. This is my own walking time, which allows for plenty of exploring and stops for scenic admiration. Should you gallop through, you can complete these walks in shorter time.

Remember not to smoke when you hike and never to litter.

Know the trail marking code:

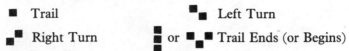

Branches or logs across a trail mean either that trail is closed or you don't want to go that way. So long as you are on a blazed trail, you are safe from trespassing. Otherwise, respect posted signs. The legend below gives the symbols used on the maps:

Ⓟ	parking area	ⵗⵗⵗ	view
• • •	main trail	—	paved road
. . . . .	side trail or alternate route	= = =	dirt road
ⵗⵕ	marsh or swamp	⭢	stream, with
▪	building		direction of flow
ⵜ	bridge	• • •	boardwalk
ⵗⵗⵗ	stone wall	○ ○ ○	bushwhack
Ψ Ψ	orchard	▲	summit
⬭	excavation	Ⱥ	lookout tower
⌐⌐	foundation	∿∿∿	vegetation boundary
⬭	pond/lake	⊂⌐⊃	fireburn area

The Inland Hills

"I'm suffocating!" cried Maryanne, who had recently moved from the Midwest to the eastern woodlands. "I can't see anything. It's claustrophobic, all these leaves!"

One hundred and fifty years ago, Maryanne would have had little to complain about. Even before Europeans came, the Native Peoples had thinned the forests with fire to encourage game and food plants, improve travel and warfare conditions, and ease the harvesting of wild plant foods. Of course, their fires were nothing compared to what the Europeans did.

To Europeans, certain trees were commodities. For instance, large old white pines, tulip trees, and northern white cedars were used in shipbuilding, and sassafras was considered a cure-all. These were scoured from what was originally a forest association of oak, white pine, chestnut, hickory, and hemlock. Hemlocks were stripped of their bark for the tanning industry and left to die. In the 1700s clear-cutting was done near sawmills along major streams. Extensive clearing made space for crops, pasture, and estate grounds, and provided fuel for the charcoal industry, the steamboats, and the railroads.

Almost all the forests of the Hudson Valley have been cut at least once. Some have been cut six, seven, or more times. After each cutting, the woods have grown back, although with each cutting, the soil has been further eroded.

Agriculture peaked in Dutchess and Putnam counties in the decade around 1875, when eighty-five to ninety percent of the land was in crops and pasture. Since then, farmland has declined steadily. The woods have grown back. Hudson Valley residents today catch glimpses through the leaves of a young-forested landscape.

But these young woods are different from the old. New species have been added, and original ones are gone. Acid rain and disease organisms have added new stresses. And in October of 1987, a heavy snowfall while the trees were in full leaf caused catastrophic damage, especially in northern Dutchess County. Those trees that survived with limb loss are now highly susceptible to disease and rot. Fifteen to twenty years from the date of the freak storm called Snowleaf, these forests will experience drastic tree failure. But inherent in natural catastrophe is rejuvenation. The dead trees will decay, releasing nutrients back into the soil for the next generation of flora.

1. Clarence Fahnestock Memorial State Park

Location: Dennytown, Putnam Valley
Distance: 2 miles; 3 to 4 hours
Owner: State of New York

In Fahnestock, one can swim, camp, fish, picnic, or rent a boat. With almost 6,200 acres, it is the largest park in Dutchess or Putnam counties. There are plenty of trails to explore. Though inland from the Hudson River, geologically the park is part of the Hudson Highlands and shares the hill region's special cold climate. Those who commute the Taconic State Parkway during the winter know that everywhere else north and south it may be raining but climb the Fahnestock plateau and it's Winter Wonderland. Expect snow on the trails until the end of March. Our route covers a remote section of the park known as the Sunken Mines.

ACCESS

From the Taconic State Parkway, exit onto NY 301 west towards Cold Spring. Go 3.1 miles, past Pelton Pond and Canopus Lake, until you see a large satellite communications tower on the hilltop in front of you. Turn left onto Dennytown Road. There will be a sign for the Taconic Outdoor Education Center. Go 1.7 miles to your first left, Sunken Mine Road, a rugged dirt road with a large sign at the entrance cautioning, "Road Closed Dec.–April 1." The road is not maintained during those months, so if you venture onto Sunken Mine Road in winter, be prepared to deal with snow, ice, and mud. Go 1.2 miles until the lake is on your left. Parking is in pull-offs. Be careful not to block the road. Phone: superintendent's office, (914) 225-7207.

TRAIL

Find the blue paint marker for the Three Lakes Trail and head toward the lake, known as John Allen Pond on old maps and, recently, as

11

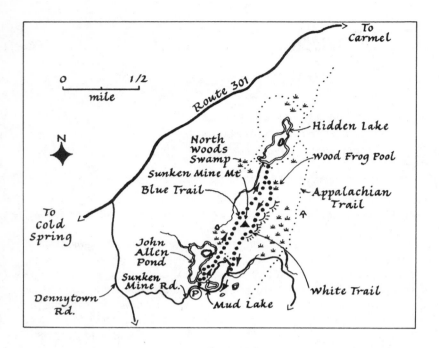

Sunken Mine Lake. Go down the slope, across Sunk Brook that waterfalls over a dam, and turn right.

The trail soon leads out on the shore of the lake at another, lower, dam. Walk the shore past bushes of swamp blueberry, *Clethra* or sweet pepperbush, mountain laurel, and sweetfern, a woody shrub with fern-like leaves. Nip off a leaf of sweetfern, crush, and smell. Native Americans nationwide have dried sweetfern for centuries. Mixed with dried tobacco and silky dogwood bark shavings, it makes a pungent smoking mixture called *kinnikinnick*, often given as a greeting gift among new or old friends.

Sweetfern indicates well-drained, dry, sandy or rocky soil. In the Hudson Valley, that means either ridge tops or river- or glacier-deposited mounds of sand, or soil that has been disturbed by human activity. The Sunken Mine area has a history of disturbance.

Soon as the area was settled and right on up to the twentieth century, the forests of Fahnestock were lumbered. The tannin in oak and hemlock bark was used to tan animal skins into leather. Wood was used for construction and for firing commercial brick kilns. Whole forests of logs were piled into great pits and slowly roasted into charcoal for home stove cooking fires and iron furnaces.

Even in colonial times, the Hudson Highlands were known to contain deposits of magnetic oxide of iron, but it wasn't until 1821 that exploratory cuts were made. In the 1860s, five mines operated on Sunken Mine Mountain. Known as the Canada Mines Group, the largest was the Sunk or Stewart Mine: 1,500 feet long and 300 feet deep. Odelltown, an entire community, flourished on Canopus Creek at the foot of Sunken Mine Mountain. A railroad on site transported the ore to NY 301 where horse and wagon carted it to the foundry at Cold Spring and then by barge to New York City.

These lumbering and mining activities changed the way the Fahnestock plateau looked. More change came with the Depression. Around 1935, the Civilian Conservation Corps dammed, among other waterways, Sunk Brook to form John Allen Pond. It is the CCC dams you walk on around this lake. Then, finally, the Sunken Mine area got a rest. Slowly, the woods have grown back.

Take the right fork that leads away from the lake, keeping an eye out for slag heaps, ditches, and old roads. They are everywhere. Fahnestock is riddled with foundations, old wells, pits, holes, cuts, charcoal heaps, ore dumps, and railroad beds. For a few yards on the blue trail, you walk on one of the old roads and, should you miss the right turn-off, you'll come to the stone foundation of a collapsed bridge. Just below this bridge, the trail passes a clump of grey beeches with bark stretched smooth as skin. Rejoin the old road and bear left at the fork.

In a half mile or so you'll come to a sunny slope of tall sugar maples and what look to be grasses. These are sedges. Feel a sedge stem. It is triangular. Grass stems are round.

Continue down the slope, turn left at the fork, and visit Hidden Lake. The trail crosses an earth dam. A strange-looking place, this lake, with all its tree stumps sticking out of the water. The slowly decomposing stumps provide a rich source of nutrients for plants and zooplankton, and the old roots provide habitat. This supports a splendid population of wildlife. Watch the water's edge for green frogs, pickerel, and bluegill. Damselfly and dragonfly adults hunt for insects in the air. Underwater, tadpoles and insect nymphs swim among water lettuce, elodea, and pickerel weed. An enormous species of ram horn snail lives here. Broken snail shells litter the shoreline. Raccoons, roving by night, locate the snails with their sensitive hands and make short work of them with their sharp teeth. Muskrats dive for the snails by day.

Each summer, female snapping turtles climb on the dam, painstakingly dig holes, and lay fifteen to fifty white, leathery, round eggs. The eggs are covered over again with sand, and you'd never know they were there unless you happened to see them hatch out. Raccoons find them, however, and each year dig for an egg feast. Infant mortality is a powerful control on reptile populations. Look for signs of this predation: disturbed sand and shriveled pieces of egg shells.

If you have time, take a quick sidetrip over the dam and turn left at the far side. Just down the path is a swamp with a wild, north woods look to it. The path—another old woods road—is lined with highbush blueberry bushes. June's the month when the berries are ripe and blue and bursting.

Return on the blue trail back up the sugar maple slope, this time bearing left onto the white trail for the return loop. If you are walking in early April, you may hear what sounds like hundreds of sticks being clacked together. You're in luck! The wood frogs are singing in the swamp pools. They gather for only two weeks to mate and then disperse back into the woods.

To see a wood frog up close, walk to the shore where the water's deep. The frogs will hear and feel you coming. They'll dive out of sight. Get seated in a position that you can hold comfortably for the next ten minutes. Lean over and put one hand in the water up to your palm. Then wait.

Wait without moving. Wait until the first wood frog resurfaces. It may take five or even ten minutes, but it's worth the patience. When one finally does resurface, keep still. Frog vision centers on movement. If you move, he'll dive. Stationary objects are ignored, so remain perfectly motionless, and more will come up. One will start to sing, then another. Finally, they'll be satisfied that you're no longer there, and they'll start in again with the racket.

A male wood frog sings by inflating two air sacs over its shoulders. He swims and glides through the open water, mounting anything his size that moves. Should he mount a receptive female, she'll lay eggs, and he'll fertilize them. More often it's an unreceptive female or another male, which results in a lot of splashing and croaking.

Once the frogs have gotten back into the swing of things, slowly move the fingers of your hand back and forth in unison. Do not move your palm. Your fingers will look the size of a frog, and the waves

14

you send out will be frog-sized. This will attract the nearest males, who will come to investigate. Let them swim onto your hand. Then you can pick them right up.

Wood frogs are brown and cinnamon, with a black mask over their gold eyes. They come to your open hand because of the Laws of Frog Behavior: If it moves and is larger than you, run from it. If it moves and is smaller than you, eat it. If it moves and is the same size as you, mate with it.

Continue along the white trail, where you will be walking just west of the brink of Sunken Mine Mountain. When you see a clear-seeming spot, bushwhack to the edge of the cliff for the view. The hemlock-studded hills pile up along the horizon, wild and windy and dark. Below you lies a steep mountain slope riddled with sunken mines, holes, shafts, adits, and pits. Please do not explore these mines. They are treacherous.

The return trail is another old mining road. Foundations lie on either side in the woods. Explore them with care. There's a narrow but deep well that you do not want to fall into. Watch for a magnificent stand of witch hazel (*Hamamelis virginiana*) on your right. These bloom in fall, when all other plants produce seeds. Once you've smelled the autumn-subtle yellow, spider-like blooms of witch hazel, you can identify its proximity simply by the honey-sweet odor in the air on a sunny day. Oil distilled from the inner bark makes a popular, sore-muscle remedy. A rod of witch hazel with a crotch is the original divining rod.

At the dirt road (Sunken Mine Road), turn around and look back the way you came. See the mine cut on the right?

Turn right onto Sunken Mine Road to return to your car. You'll pass Mud Pond. Be sure to see the painted turtles and spotted newts.

2. Walter G. Merritt Park

Location: Haviland Hollow
Distance: 4 miles; 3 hours
Owner: County of Putnam

This is a brand-new park, still in the planning stage. Currently, a trail leads to the hemlock ravine and gorge of Tucker's Run, then connects with scenic Stage Coach Road to the south, which was abandoned by the town because the hemlock gorge it follows is precipitous. The loop ends with a tramp along Haviland Hollow Road.

ACCESS

From NY 22, turn east onto Haviland Hollow Road/Putnam County 68 and drive 2.3 miles. Parking is on the left just before a small bridge as you enter a valley. At present, this park is open to the general public. Phone: County Clerk, (914) 225-3641, ext. 302, or County Planning, (914) 878-3480.

TRAIL

The trail begins along an old road. In April, the delicious white bulbs of wild leek (*Allium tricoccum*) push up smooth green leaves on purple stems just when the shadflies appear. (Should the flies bother you, munch on a leaf or two of the wild leek. Out from your pores will exude a natural insect repellent.) Sensitive to the heat of summer, the leaves of wild leek die by June. The white flower umbels bloom in June and July. Soon after that, the flowers die, and all that remains are the cloves of the bulbs barely sticking up out of the ground.

The trail veers left uphill alongside the stone walls of an old farmstead, past many deer trails and well-browsed juniper. The trail levels and follows the ridge slope through a mixed deciduous forest of sugar maple, shagbark and pignut hickory, ash, and tulip. In the wet areas of intermittent streams grows spicebush, which blooms in late April at the same time that Japanese barberry is just leafing out.

16

In late April, the spear-long buds of beech trees swell, loosening the gold scales that protected the embryonic leaves and flowers during the winter. The scales are pushed open and fall to the ground. As May progresses, an entire new branch of leaves grows out from that bud. I am always amazed by how fast this happens, how rapidly the tree buds break open and the trees leaf out. In a week's time, the landscape changes from grey, open branches and trunks to a green wall of softness.

The trail leads to the hemlock and striped maple (*Acer pensylvanicum*) gorge of Tucker's Run, similar to the gorge at Pawling Preserve, but larger, and full of falls and cataracts. At the intersection, turn left along an old road and follow upstream past pools and cascades. Watch for the foundation of an old stone bridge. On either bank is built a retaining wall, and on the opposite side you can make out roads, one that went upstream, the other downstream. Just above this bridge, Tucker's Run rushes over a sill of bedrock into an emerald-deep pool.

When the road swings left and away from the stream, stay on the

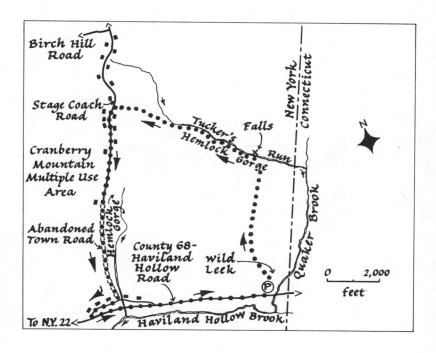

Japanese barberry.

trail along the bank, and the road will reappear. Another brook bubbles in from the left. The trail continues upstream as the hemlocks gradually disappear, the stream levels, and the forest becomes mixed deciduous. The path may become obscure. This portion of the trail may be rerouted, as some sections may cross onto private property. Should the trail eventually be closed, you can always bushwhack.

At Stage Coach Road, turn left. This is the old stage route that connected Danbury to Boston, with an overnight stop at the Quaker Hill Church and stables. Pass Cranberry Mountain Multiple Use Area and houses. The last house is an old one. Its stone retaining wall has rough steps built in its face for passengers to dismount from the stage coach. Just beyond this house Stage Coach Road becomes an official abandoned town road and the hemlock gorge begins.

It is said the road into the ravine was closed after two cars met one night. Unable to pass, some of the cars' occupants got out to help one vehicle back down the road. One person fell off the unprotected edge and rolled down the ravine, injuring himself severely. The posted speed limit still stands: 5 MPH. Grassy and beautiful, the road tilts steeply downhill into Haviland Hollow, known locally simply as The Hollow. At the paved road, turn *right. Do not turn left,* as that road is private property. At Haviland Hollow Road, turn left for a one mile tramp to your car.

3. Stony Kill Farm Environmental Education Center

Location: Chelsea
Distance: 2 miles; 2 hours
Owner: State of New York

NY 9D bisects the 756-acre Stony Kill Farm, the homestead (originally 1,000 acres) of one branch of Gulian Verplanck's descendants. The farm was handed down through generations of Verplancks until 1942. The 1836 Manor House, 1740 Stone House, farm buildings, educational exhibits, and the Verplanck Trail lie on the west side. Our walk is on the east side where the land has been farmed continuously for the past 300 years, only recently left to run wild. The woods have grown back in the typical fashion of a suburban regrowth bottomland forest of the Hudson Valley, the perfect place to learn about backyard ecology.

ACCESS

Stony Kill Farm is located between Beacon and Wappingers Falls on NY 9D. From Beacon, take NY 9D north past Chelsea Ridge Park. At the traffic light, turn right onto Red Schoolhouse Road. From Wappingers Falls, go south on NY 9D past Hughsonville and Baxtertown Road to a left at the light onto Red Schoolhouse Road. On Red Schoolhouse Road, go 0.2 miles to a dirt driveway on the left. Park in the field. Should the gate be shut, you can park at the Manor House and walk over on the white trail. Phone: park office, (914) 831-8780.

TRAIL

The Sierra Trail, level for nearly all its two miles, begins as a dirt road at the end of the meadow. This is an old cow path, which was used for centuries. When you step under the shade of trees, watch for the white trail on your left that leads across NY 9D to the Manor House. Thirty feet past this intersection on the left grows a swamp white oak—majestic, tall, and lopsided. There are practically no branches on the left side, but on the right the limbs stretch so far they overhang the trail, and the trunk leans so that you'd swear one good blow would knock it down. Oaks will reach for full sunlight as far as gravity allows. When you see a large old tree with low slung branches in a forest, you know as a young sapling it grew in a field where it had the sunlight to itself. When it grows lopsided, it grew on the edge of a forest out into the sunlight of an open pasture.

At the T intersection, the trail is covered with the round leaves and the maroon-tipped stems of plantain (*Plantago major*). A medicinal plant brought to America by European colonists, plantain escaped the herbal garden and today plagues suburban lawn-owners nationwide. They should be happy they've got it. Plantain is the cure for the kind of shallow skin-scrape kids get when they skid on pavement. Four plantain leaves folded, scrubbed on concrete to extract the juices, and

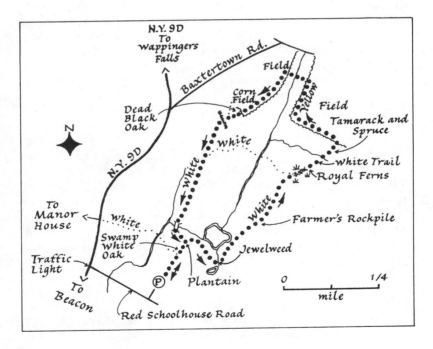

applied to the hurt for ten minutes cures the pain and the swelling. No kidding.

Last summer I tubed the Esopus River, and my friends and I suffered the common mishaps of bruised shins and elbows. I plucked plantain leaves on the shore (the stuff grows almost everywhere there's sun) and set-up a first aid station just below the Colorado Rapids run. The wounded thought the plantain cure miraculous. Bad bruises that would have pained them for days were relieved in minutes, with only a little redness to show their disbelieving co-workers at the office the next day.

For an old country trick, pluck a plantain with stem intact. Notice how the veins run close to the underside of the leaf, and how this underside looks like the hull of a wooden boat. Hold it in your palm top side up. With a fingernail, cut through the leaf at the base just above the stem, stopping at the veins. Carefully, pull the stem from the leaf. With practice, you'll stretch the veins out, and you've got a miniature fiddle.

Take the right fork and follow the white trail past the ponds. Enter the woods and cross a brook. Here grow jewelweed and spicebush, indicators of wet or poorly-drained soil or moist, rich forest soil. Jewelweed stems are green and translucent, like glass tubes, with swellings at the nodes where the leaves sprout from the stem, and a purple base at the roots.

Pluck a jewelweed leaf, careful not to touch anything but the stem, and hold the leaf under water. Twirl it. The leaf turns as silver-bright as aluminum foil. Take the leaf out; it will be completely dry. This works even better in a clear glass of water held up in the sunlight or in a sunny pond.

Jewelweed is also called touch-me-not. The jewels of yellow (*Impatiens pallida*) or orange (*I. capensis*) flowers ripen into green pods. When ready, the pod walls turn translucent; you can see the black seeds inside. Touch the fat pod and pop! it explodes. The seeds wing away in all directions, propelled by a coiled green spring.

The old country trick is to pluck a bursting-ripe jewelweed pod without exploding it, take it to a city friend, and tell them to close their eyes and put out their hand.

Up the tree trunks climbs poison ivy lush and oily with urushiol acid. Should you touch poison ivy and get the toxin on your skin, don't wait until you get home to scrub with brown soap and smear on the calamine. Pick a large jewelweed, slit the glass-tube stem, and

The author demonstrating how to make a plantain fiddle on a nature walk. The participants are hard at work making their own.

apply the ample juice. For most folks, this counteracts the toxin. Apply several times a day to dry up established poison ivy cases.

Walk the woods of red, black, white, and pin oak, red maple, tulip, and beech. Throughout these woods grows a tree with a trunk like a muscled arm. This is ironwood (*Carpinus caroliniana*), and as its name implies, it resists hammer and nails.

As you walk, listen for a high sharp bird chirp, sometimes repeated incessantly. This is chipmunk, the only ground squirrel of the eastern woodlands. Listen also for the many songbirds that live in these woods, especially the waterfall notes of the veery.

The white trail turns left for the return loop of one mile. If you wish to continue for the full two miles, keep straight on the yellow trail. Be forewarned that portions of the yellow trail may be difficult if not impossible to find in summer. Go down a slight slope that curves left. Straight before you stands a young sycamore with blue, grey, green, and brown bark-scabs set against a smooth pale blue-white skin.

A rock and corduroy bridge crosses a red maple swamp. Look for the royal ferns, indicators of wetlands. The fern is a rare plant and is protected by New York State law. On the surface of the mud and the dead pools of water floats an oil slick. This is marsh gas, a natural by-product of bacterial decay in an anaerobic, or nonoxygen, environment. Smelly but indicative of a healthy swamp. Shortly after crossing a stone wall, enter a stand of white pine, Norway spruce, and tamarack. This was once a nursery.

Hear the crickets ahead? Cross a stone wall and walk out under the wide, bright green canopy of a young hickory into the field. The trail turns left and follows the field edge.

In summer, many plant stems are globbed with spit. Grasshoppers and snakes get blamed for this, but if you explore inside a glob (not so disgusting as you think), you'll find a spittlebug nymph. Early in the morning, the spittlebug, soft-bodied, green, with two red dots for eyes, exudes two chemical secretions that combine to form a liquid waxy soap. Dipping its abdomen tip into the soap, it bubbles the soap up until it is surrounded with a cool foamy nest in which to spend the day. The sweet smelling spittle attracts small insects. They wade into the spit and into the waiting jaws of the spittlebug.

Follow the field edges with care; the ground is uneven from generations of plowing. Red clover, yarrow, hawkweed, bouncing Bet, buttercup, and milkweed are only a few of the native and alien species that bloom among the many species of grasses. Enter woods, cross a stone wall and an intermittent stream, and emerge into more fields. Halfway through, the ground is plowed and planted each year with Stony Kill's tallest grass species, corn. Reenter the forest. The white trail rejoins the yellow. Cross the bridge over the pond's outlet and you're back at the T intersection and your car.

4. Pawling Nature Preserve

Location: Pawling
Distance: 1 mile; 1 to 2 hours
Owner: The Nature Conservancy

The Pawling Preserve spans Hammersley Ridge, part of the north-to-south running wall of the Harlem Valley. It is a large place, 1,015 acres, and there are many trails to walk besides the short loop described in this chapter. Nominated as a National Natural Landmark by the U.S. Department of Interior, Pawling Preserve contains a diverse cross section of natural habitats characteristic of eastern New York. Rare, threatened, and endangered species of plants and animals live here, including a large number of songbird species.

ACCESS

From Pawling, take NY 22 north about 2 miles. Turn east onto Dutchess County 68/North Quaker Hill Road. At the fork (Hurds Corners), bear right up the hill to a left onto Quaker Lake Road. Go 1.3 miles. Quaker Lake Road turns to dirt at the lake, sometimes very muddy in spring. Continue past the lake for 0.75 mile. Trailhead parking on the left. Phone: the Nature Conservancy's Lower Hudson Chapter office in Katonah, (914) 232-9431. To prevent overgrazing, there is a limited deer hunting season that lasts for about three weeks in autumn, at which time the park is closed. No dogs are allowed at any time.

TRAIL

Follow the trail to the sound of rushing water for a view of the gorge. In the channel below this cool hemlock ravine nests the Acadian flycatcher, the Louisiana waterthrush, and the winter wren. The winter wren is a northern bird. Pawling Preserve lies near the southern border of its summer range at this elevation. It is also one of only a few places in Dutchess County where the Acadian flycatcher breeds.

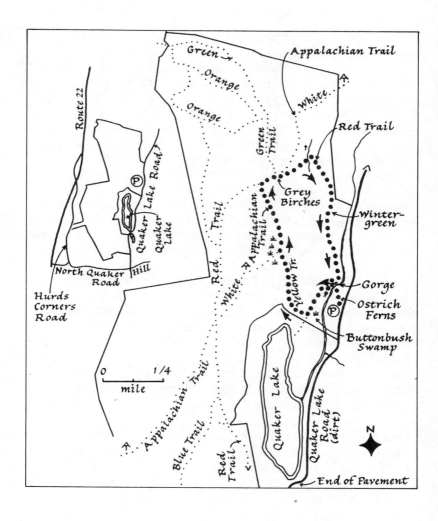

The ravine bedrock is a micaceous, or mica-bearing, schist veined with marble. The limestone that weathers from the marble into the soil and the cool, moist microclimate of the ravine combine to support a unique fern community among the rocks: bladder fern, bulblet fern, fragile fern, walking fern, maidenhair spleenwort, and silvery spleenwort. The soil bank of the stream is cloaked with liverworts. Back on the trail, stop on the footbridge and take a look at the brook. Shiny flakes of mica sparkle in the sand and gravel of the brook bed. Whole slabs of mica-schist gleam under the water.

Cross the stone wall and go straight on the yellow trail. Climb the ravine wall under hemlocks and white pines. Hemlocks (*Tsuga canadensis*) grow and tend to persist on slopes in southern New York where it is cool and moist year-round. In traditional ecological terms, such a growth was called a climax forest: self-perpetuating and stable unless some catastrophe (such as a blowdown or a bulldozer) occurred. However, in recent years the climax theory has been found to be misleading because it is too generalized and static a concept to describe the dynamic and complex nature of systems. Ecologists tend to be more cautious in forecasting future vegetative trends in a given site, knowing that many things must be taken into account, including bedrock, soil, climate and microclimate, history, chance, fire, animal grazing, wind damage, moisture, and human activities—to name just a few.

In colonial times hemlocks were heavily harvested. Their bark, which is high in tannin, was stripped from the trees for use in the skin-tanning industry. Native Americans used hemlock for its astringent properties. Hemlock is an astringent, stronger than a lemon. Hemlock tea bathed on a wound puckers it closed and stops the bleeding. Hemlock needle tea drunk puckers the mouth, the esophagus, the stomach lining, the intestinal lining, and is still strong enough to tighten the large intestine and stop severe diarrhea. Powerful stuff. Taken as a weak tea or munched raw, hemlock needles supply vitamin C.

Some of the hemlocks here are giants. This species can live for up to six centuries. It is so dark beneath their needles that few if any shrubs or herbaceous plants can grow. A dense hemlock canopy allows less than twenty percent of a day's full sunlight to penetrate to the forest floor. This enhances humidity and coolness. In such shade is found only sapling and seedling hemlocks, but even they cannot flourish without sunlight. Although extremely shade-tolerant, a shaded hemlock grows slowly. Trees no thicker than a broom handle may be fifty years old. Should there come a blow-down that opens the overhead canopy to let in the full sunlight, that fifty-year old hemlock will shoot up, growing faster in a few summers than in all its fifty years. This is one of the adaptations that make hemlock a dominant species.

While you can still hear the falls of the gorge, watch on your right for a mica-schist overhang large enough to walk beneath. This was a rock shelter used by archaic and woodland Indians during hunting expeditions thousands of years ago. Several species of lichens and mosses coat the rock.

The trail levels off and the hemlocks abruptly end. Slight differences in annual mean temperature, water availability, and soil composition cause to develop a different association of tree species. The soil here is thicker and warmer and the slope no longer so steep. Here grow oaks and sugar maples in a mesic, or medium moist, soil environment.

And here lies the buttonbush swamp. Buttonbushes (*Cephalanthus occidentalis*) grow in the standing water. Few plants have round flower clusters, but buttonbush blooms are perfect spheres, clusters of cream flowers so sweet smelling the shrub's old country name is honey balls. The fruits develop from the globe, and these balls hang from the twigs far into the winter.

Continue on the yellow trail until you come to the white-blazed Appalachian Trail, where you turn right. All through the park one finds dead juniper, or red cedar. Dead and dying grey birches lie at the intersection of the green trail with the Appalachian. This area was cleared and farmed in the past. True, it is possible to find some healthy junipers and grey birches, but they are doomed. Grey birch and juniper are pioneer species that colonize open fields. They grow swiftly in the open sunlight, a harsh dry environment of extreme temperatures that many other tree species cannot survive. Shade is cast beneath the juniper and grey birch branches. Humidity is trapped. In that humid shade their own young, who need full sunlight, cannot grow. Intead, shade-tolerant sugar maple and oak sprout and thrive. The maple and oak trees grow taller than any grey birch or juniper, overtop them, shut out their full sunlight, and so kill them.

The trunks of the dead junipers and the white-barked bodies of the grey birches tell us that this was once an open field. This vegetational change that begins with a field of cleared forest and proceeds to return to forest is one example of a process called succession. Each stage in the process paves the way to the next. In effect, each stage dooms itself.

Bear right onto the red trail. Here is a wet area of red maple, ash, spicebush, and sensitive fern, and the trail is usually muddy. Bedrock lies close to the surface. Even though we're on top of the ridge, the water has nowhere to go and simply stays put. Red maple and ash can tolerate this wetness, exposure, and thin soil that disfavor other trees, and therefore are dominant on this site.

Continue for the descent off the ridge. As with the ascent, we traverse a mesic slope of red oak, tulip tree, black cherry, and sugar maple. On your right will be one lone paper birch. Should you walk this route when the leaves are down, you get a beautiful view of the ridges and the steep valley wall.

Cross a brook and start up a knoll. Bedrock outcrops appear, covered with lichens and mosses. The soil layer thins to mere millimeters. The sugar maple and the red oak end, to be replaced by scrub and chestnut oak, white pine, mountain laurel, and lowbush blueberry.

This is a dry, or xeric, upland soil site where the bedrock is close to and at the soil surface. In the red maple site, the bedrock formed a sort of dishpan that trapped and held the water. But here, even though we are at a lower elevation, the bedrock is shaped as a peak, and the water runs right off. All year round, the soil stays dry. A xeric-condition-adapted scrub oak or chestnut oak can outcompete any sugar maple or red oak in this spot. One pitch pine stands in the path with a trail marker tacked to it. This pine has three needles per cluster, whereas white pine has five. Pitch pine is adapted to growing in near-desert conditions, although it also grows in bogs!

Watch along the ground for a small evergreen plant that looks like infant mountain laurel. This is wintergreen (*Gaultheria procumbens*). Pinch off a tiny bit of leaf, and you'll smell the methyl salicylate that made nineteenth-century medicine flavorings famous (or, should we say, infamous).

Beside the trail on the right grows a large clump of several species of reindeer lichens, common in the tundra of Canada. The trail winds downhill along the ravine wall. The soil becomes moist and the climate cool, and you're back in the hemlocks. Rejoin the yellow trail just above the gorge for the return to your car.

5. Thomas J. Boyce Park

Location: Wingdale
Distance: Almost 3 miles; 2 to 3 hours
Owner: Town of Dover

The town of Dover consists of two long north-south ridges and a valley: West Mountain, East Mountain (which separates New York from Connecticut), and the Harlem Valley in between. This corridor continues north into Columbia County.

Boyce Park lies just south of East Mountain proper. It is a 199-acre municipal recreation facility with the added bonus of a hill that forms part of the Harlem Valley wall—a 1,126 foot escarpment with one hell of a view.

ACCESS

Boyce Park is on the east side of NY 55 just north of the intersection with NY 22 and Dutchess County 21. Just to the south is Harlem Valley State Hospital. Webatuck is just to the north. Phone: Dover Town Clerk, (914) 832-6111.

TRAIL

Stand a moment and look around. A gravel road heads for the back hay field, an escarpment rises behind. What's on top, a cleared area? What's that, a platform? The hangliders' platform. Our destination.

The gravel road is eroded in spots. The ruts are filled with sand, gravel, and cobbles. The Harlem Valley is choked with glacial outwash. If you drive around the area, you will see many mining operations digging up what the last glacier dumped.

Also in the gravel road are iridescent black rough rocks. These are the end-products of burning coal from Harlem Valley Hospital's coal-burning plant. Cinders are useful road-building material.

Keep on the gravel road. A view of the escarpment when the leaves are down clearly shows a stratification of tree species. The dark green

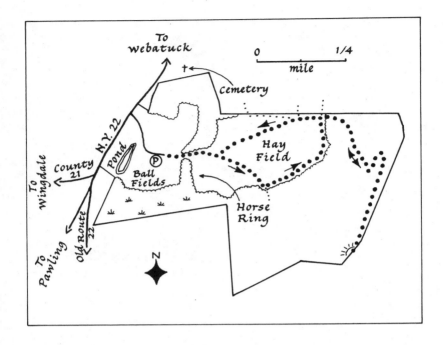

evergreens toward the top are hemlock. The mid-section of the slope grows bone-white paper birch. They look like giant nerve endings. Across the base grow brown-tipped tulip trees. The brown tips are the dried seed heads.

The road forks. Follow the fork of your choice past nesting bobolinks to the field's northeasternmost corner, where the road enters the woods and begins its ascent. It's a steep climb.

The hangliders' platform is not the summit but close enough. What a view! It's a long way down to that hay field, especially if you're flinging yourself off the platform with a giant kite. If it felt breezy below, the wind's terrific up here. The tops of hills bear the brunts of storms, and to such storms the hilltop flora and fauna must be adapted.

There spreads the Harlem Valley, a calcite and dolomite marble trough deep in alkaline soils and glacial outwash. Many of the limey farm fields are abandoned and being colonized by either red cedar or family housing projects. See the round turquoise water tank to your right? Those evergreens around it are all red cedar (*Juniperus virgi-*

niana), a forest of them, typical on calcareous old pastures. Their tops are pointed, and they are brown-green in winter, turning bright dark green in summer. They grow all over the valley where once there were fields. Gosh, that's a lot of abandoned farmland. The cedars in the cemetery are rounded on top and greener in winter. These are planted northern white cedars (*Thuja occidentalis*). The dark green evergreens on the upper slopes of the hills are hemlocks. On West Mountain, some of the dark conifers are white and pitch pines.

Straight ahead is Sharparoon, south of the power line. The Catskills peek behind. The Swamp River meanders below. To the north it joins the Ten Mile River.

The Harlem Valley's carbonate bedrock overlain by sand and gravel allows rainwater to percolate through at a high rate into the ground water. You are looking at an aquifer, a place where ground water is recharged and purified. Not a place to seal with blacktop or dump full of toxins. It is said that Dover has the purest water in New York State. So pure is it that, as a public drinking supply, it need not be chlorinated.

The high spots in the valley floor are marble bedrock outcrops or, plainly put, marble hills, where rare plants grow. These hills are what gave Dover its name, after the white cliffs of Dover in England. The ridge walls of East and West Mountain are made mostly of more resistant schists with some phyllites where rare timber rattlesnakes live.

The Harlem Valley division of the New York Central Railroad was completed in 1850. It was one of the first railroads in the country, and the oldest that leads to Manhattan.

It was the Harlem Valley Railroad that put an end to the livestock drives. Farmers in Vermont and the northern states drove thousands of cattle, sheep, and other livestock south to New York City for slaughter via the Harlem Valley. Monday was market day in the city, and as many as 2,000 head of cattle could be seen on the road between Dover and Pawling at the end of most weeks. With so much livestock moving through, taverns for the thirsty drovers flourished. Old Drover's Inn in Dover is all that remains.

Return the way you came. You can vary the walk through the hay field by taking a different road fork.

6. Tymor Forest

Location: Union Vale
Distance: 3 miles; 2 hours
Owner: Town of Union Vale

In 1971, Ralph and Jean Connor donated the 500-acre Tymor Forest to the Town of Union Vale as a municipal park. This little jewel contains more than the usual ball fields and playgrounds. In one short loop, half of which is along an old nineteenth-century road, the walker visits fields, deciduous and conifer woods, Clove Creek, a hemlock ravine, cataracts, Furnace Pond, the remains of a lime mill and iron furnace, and limestone outcrops on which grow rare plants.

Until now, Tymor has been open only to Union Vale residents. Town and recreation board officials have kindly allowed the park's inclusion in this book. However, there are restrictions for nonresidents. Tymor is open to the general public only after Labor Day until Memorial Day and is closed all summer. At all times, all recreational facilities and buildings are strictly off-limits.

ACCESS

From the Taconic State Parkway, take NY 55 east, past the Billings light to the intersection with East Noxon and Bruzgul Roads. Turn left or east onto Bruzgul. Drive 1.7 miles. As you come down the mountain, you'll see a wide valley with fields. The white farm buildings are Tymor Forest. At the row of red pines, turn right onto Duncan Road. Turn at your first left. Park at the silos. Phone: Union Vale Town Clerk, (914) 724-5600.

TRAIL

Walk along the road toward the stream. This is Clove Creek, which drains The Clove, the valley you saw as you drove down the mountain. The Clove runs north-south from Beekman through Union Vale. Since colonial days, it has supported a rich farming community. The west wall of The Clove is called Clove Mountain, and sometimes West

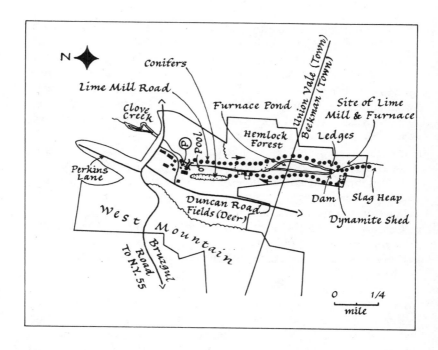

Mountain, and the east wall is East Mountain—which might be confusing when you travel over East Mountain to the Harlem Valley, where The Clove's East Mountain becomes West Mountain.

Keep outside the split-rail fence, past the large old red maple, and along the creek into a picnic area. Clove Creek waterfalls over the remains of a dam near the site of a grist mill. Built very early, the mill ground flour until 1925, when it was torn down. There was a hamlet here, at the junction of Bruzgul and Lime Mill Roads and Clove Creek, called Crouse's Store. Beer's 1867 map shows the mill as both a grist- and a sawmill, with a few homes nearby, Mr. D.A. Crouse's store, and, inside the store—the sure sign of a regional center—a post office. Keep on through the picnic area to an old bridge, dated with a marble slab: "Erected 1910." You are on Lime Mill Road.

Redwings, robins, and grackles call along the creek and from the old corn meadow. Try the "spishing call" (see Bowdoin Park chapter) as you walk this road bounded on both sides by ecotones. Pass two old white oaks on the right and enter hemlocks. The Connors planted the white pine plantation on your left. Clove Creek curves and speeds up. Leave Lime Mill Road at the sidetrail and follow the creek bank to a view of the top of the gorge. Resist the temptation to clamber up the steep hemlock slope and range along the rocks. The shallow root systems of hemlock are fatally susceptible to the compaction caused by trampling, and compaction on such a steep slope with little vegetation to hold the soil causes severe erosion. Return to Lime Mill Road. We'll see more of the gorge shortly.

The hemlock forest on your left is deep and dark and beautiful. Leave the road and loop through it if you wish. There is a long narrow sill of grooved and eroded limestone on the forest floor that makes one fantasize of caves hollowed beneath Tymor Park. Lime Mill Road follows on top the ravine wall.

Centuries ago, the hemlock-cool Clove Creek gorge continued, but now the creek slows and quiets as it enters Furnace Pond. On your right is an old metal gate through which a side trail leads to the bottom of the rapids.

At Furnace Pond, take a look inside the boathouse at the rafters where mud dauber or pipe organ wasps have built their mud nests. Inside each tube mother wasp lays an egg. You may see her enter with a spider held in her legs. She stuffs the spider, paralyzed with her preservative sting, into the tube. When the pipe organ is well provisioned with powerless spiders, she seals it shut. Left to itself, the egg hatches into a wasp larva that feeds on the paralyzed food. The larva grows, metamorphoses into an adult, chews its way through the mud nest, and flies free.

Lime Mill Road follows the edge of Furnace Pond, past red osier dogwood and speckled alder. In early May, the powder blue, spring azure butterfly dances on Lime Mill Road and in the woods. When abreast of the southern end of the hemlock island, the road begins a slight uphill climb. A sidetrail on your right leads to the ledges.

The sidetrail hugs the bank. At the fork, choose the upper path. You are walking past outcroppings of limestone, an alkaline environment common in The Clove and the Harlem Valley. (Lime belts are found elsewhere in Dutchess County, especially in East Fishkill and Pine Plains.) Since most of the bedrock and soils in Dutchess and Putnam Counties are acidic, the presence of alkaline limestone bedrock and the carbonate soil that weathers from that bedrock allows plants with limited acidity tolerance to grow. Watch for roundleaf hepatica (*Hepatica americana*), lyre-leaved rock cress (*Arabis lyrata*), smooth rock cress (*A. laevigata*), pussytoes (*Antennaria* sp.), early saxifrage (*Saxifraga virginiensis*), wild ginger (*Asarum canadense*), rue anemone (*Anemonella thalictroides*), columbine (*Aquilegia canadensis*), and the tiny maidenhair spleenwort fern (*Asplenium Trichomanes*). Many of these are May blooming flowers that go dormant or senescent, drying up and disappearing for the remainder of the growing season. The red-osier dogwoods and bladdernut bushes we see throughout Tymor Forest further suggest a limey soil. Among all these plants live small land snails that use the calcium found in the plants and soil to grow their shells. These snails blend in so well that they are difficult to spot, but you might find a white-bleached spiral shell from one that died.

Just before the sidetrail intersects the road at the dam, look on your left for the quarry. Upon the ground lie a few marble blocks, well-pitted from decades of rainfall.

The granite-gneiss mountains that border The Clove and even The Clove itself were rich in iron ore deposits, especially hematite with a large proportion of what is called "ochery or fine ore" on old mining reports, more valuable than other ore varieties. Several pit mines operated in today's towns of Beekman and Union Vale. In 1831 below the dam of Furnace Pond, Elisha Sterling and Co. built a charcoal-fired, iron-smelting furnace called the Beekman furnace. The hamlet

Hepatica.

of Beekman Furnace just downstream grew so large it was renamed Clove Valley. It had a population of two hundred mostly iron company employees. Clove Mountain and The Clove's East Mountain soon were clear-cut and their forests roasted into charcoal. By 1873, Clove Valley contained the Clove Spring Iron Works, and Mr. Sterling had added an anthracite-fired furnace slightly to the south.

In the 1880s, the iron industry in the Hudson Valley ended. The old charcoal-fueled Beekman furnace was torn down, its stones used to build the dam at Furnace Pond. A lime mill was built, powered by the fall of water. The anthracite-powered Beekman furnace stack still stands on Furnace Road, on private property where it is unwanted and has not long to last.

Walk downstream. The numerous foundations, sluiceway, and pipe are the remains of the lime mill that gave Lime Mill Road its name. Operated until the 1930s, the mill supplied farmers with pulverized alkaline lime to neutralize or sweeten their acidic fields, the better to make the crops grow.

Cross the bridge to the limestone quarry where there is a stone barbecue. The yellow trail turns right. Keep straight on the dirt road for the slag heap.

Here was dumped a mountain of slag: molten limestone that combined with the impurities melting out from the iron ore inside the Beekman furnace. Much of it looks like turquoise obsidian. For decades, wagons and then trucks filled their flatbeds with this slag and carted it off. Excellent landfill, the slag underlies driveways, roads, houses, and churches, nearly all the older properties of the surrounding towns.

Return to the yellow trail, which climbs steeply uphill past the wood ruin of the dynamite shed and between a pair of huge old white oaks. When you come to the field, keep along the pond edge. The trail ducks under the hemlocks to the water's brink. Ironwoods, chewed years ago by beaver (see the teeth marks?) are resprouting. Beaver rarely decimate a woods. Whatever they chew tends to resprout.

The yellow trail climbs steeply uphill, then downhill under hemlocks, then along the gorge. When you come to the lawn, you can see Clove Mountain straight ahead, once again grown over with forest and topped by a New York State firetower. At the fence, keep left to return to your car.

7. James Baird State Park

Location: Freedom Plains, LaGrange
Distance: 3.3 miles; 2 hours
Owner: State of New York

Fifty years ago, contractor James Baird donated his farm to become a recreational state park. Further land acquisitions brought the park to a total of 590 acres that today includes a golf course, a swimming pool, picnic areas, tennis courts, and ball playing fields. There's even a restaurant. The hills have been left wooded, and the moss-grown trails cross a landscape of undulating knolls and ravines, brooks, woodland pools, and moss-covered outcrops of bedrock. In this park we see the red cedar or juniper in all stages of its life cycle.

ACCESS

James Baird State Park has its own exit off the Taconic State Parkway just north of the NY 55 exit. There is another entrance from Freedom Road. Park at the restaurant. Phone: park office, (914) 452-1489.

TRAIL

Look at the sizes of the junipers (*Juniperus virginiana*) in the parking lot. They are seldom so tall, gnarled, and mature in a forest. Junipers require full sunlight. In the parking lot, they get it. No deciduous sapling is allowed to overtop them, and the junipers have matured to a miraculous size. In autumn and winter, they have waxy blue berries. Keep some in your pocket, and the cedar-fresh smell will be with you for months. Put juniper berries in a crock with sugar and grain to ferment into sock-knocking gin.

Juniper is also called red cedar because of its aromatic red heartwood that people build into chests and closets to repel clothes moths. Among Native Americans, cedar is a powerful purification and spiritual plant.

Search the branches and you will find the cedar apple gall, the fruit of the rust fungus *Gymnosporangium globoscum*, which alternates its

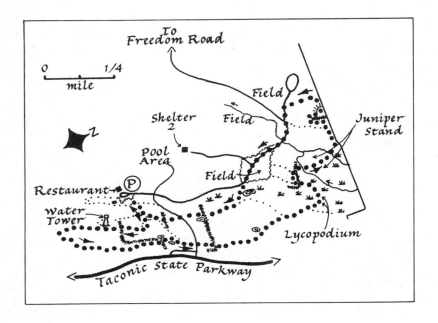

years between juniper and apple and plum trees. After a warm rain in May, fleshy orange strings exude from these "cedar apples," mature, and release spores, which next infest apple trees, causing brown scabs on the apples. In an attempt to keep their trees free from this rust fungus, orchard owners kill all junipers near their orchards. If no apples grow near an infected juniper, *Gymnosporangium globoscum* will host on any member of the rose family.

Go east from the parking lot across the road and to the left edge of the lawn where a trail leads uphill.

In the woods, the junipers grow as tall as those in the parking lot. They are probably the same age, yet only their crowns are alive with needles, the only place where they get sunlight. The scraggly things are crowded close. Deciduous species are overtopping them. Already, many of these junipers are dead. Soon, all will die. But this is no tragic thing. A short moment in the sun is the juniper's niche as a field pioneer species.

White pines (*Pinus strobus*) grow throughout Baird Park's forest. As with junipers, white pines require full sunlight, and grow their needles only at the crown in the full sunlight of the forest canopy. The limbs below in the shade are dead. But, unlike the juniper, these white pines are healthy and will live a long time. White pine is a dominant species in the north woods of New England. It grows as tall as (often taller than) any deciduous tree, and can reach the sunlight it needs. At one time, white pine was an important component of Dutchess County forests, but debarking for the tanning industry reduced its numbers drastically.

Throughout the forest we will see hemlock. This climax conifer is shade-tolerant to the extreme. You'll find its lower limbs all alive and dark with needles. So here in one park, we see three conifers, red cedar, white pine, and hemlock, with three different adaptations to climate and light.

At the dirt road turn left, go about twenty feet and take the right fork, then the left. At the four-way intersection, a sort of triangle, keep straight and to the right. Pass the wood stave water tower. In winter, the views through the leafless oaks show fields and hills. Sedimentary layers of clay metamorphosed into red and green slate bend and fold in the bedrock outcrops, shot through with veins of weathered quartz. Chestnut oak predominates in the highest, driest sites.

Search the trunks for the yellow, flannel-covered eggs of gypsy moth. Near these eggs can usually be found the fat brown pupae cases, hollow and crackling, and a few shriveled skins shed by the growing larvae or caterpillars. When in 1869 those eight gypsy moth larvae from Germany, adapted to cyclical defoliations of their native oaks in the Black Forest, escaped their blown-over cage in Medford and crawled off into the oak woods of Massachusetts, they became the classic example of a successful alien species gone wild in a new frontier. With no predator to check them, an amicable climate, and a ready food supply, the gypsy moth population mushroomed. Millions of dollars were spent to spray the Hudson Valley with tons of DDT to halt the gypsy moth. The effort failed miserably, poisoning our ecosystem and helping to eliminate raptors from the region. Gypsy moths overpopulate and defoliate the oak forests of their native Germany every seven or so years. They do the same in New York. True, some oaks died in those first years of invasion, but the oak-dominant forests of the Hudson Valley have adjusted to the gypsy moth, and both are here to stay.

Some of the egg cases you find may have a pinpoint hole in each pearl-hard egg. This is the mark of a parasitic wasp. The U.S. Department of Agriculture imported *Ooencyrtus kuwanai,* and other parasites, as a more natural control on the gypsy moth. The tiny female wasp injects her egg into the gypsy moth egg. Upon hatching, the wasp larva eats the moth egg larva. Come spring, out hatches a parasitic wasp rather than a gypsy moth caterpillar.

Keep straight across the paved entrance road. At the fork turn right, then left at the next fork. Princess pine (*Lycopodium obscurum*), a club moss, grows on both sides of the trail. Take the right fork past the ground cedar (*L. complanatum*) to a field of juniper and poverty grass. Turn right. Cross a brook and enter a dense juniper stand, young enough to be thriving. At the next fork keep straight/right. The trail curves around a bedrock outcrop topped by one of the farm's original stone walls. The trail tops a knoll where there is another view of fields and hills through the trees. In winter, you may hear the Canada geese; hundreds of them often rest nights on the golf course, winging away each dawn to feed and returning at dusk.

Follow through fields of young juniper, poverty grass, goldenrod, and ground cedar *lycopodium.* At the road turn left, and left again at the paved road. Watch for juniper seedlings beginning the successional cycle from field to forest as they take root in the bank of the road. Just past the Shelter Two picnic area, watch for the trail on the left. Follow it to the junction. Turn right, cross the paved road, and keep right again at the triangle intersection.

8. Sharparoon

Location: Dover
Distance: 8.5 miles; 6 to 8 hours
Owner: New York City Mission Society

After decades of farming and a lively iron mining and smelting history, Sharparoon Pond and its nearby, intact 1800s iron furnace, iron mines, and charcoal pits were purchased in 1922 by the New York City Mission Society as a summer camp for New York City boys. Land purchases continued, so that today the Society owns nearly 2,000 acres of forests, streams, and ponds in the Harlem Valley and along the Swamp River and West Mountain. Presently, there are two camps on the property. Camp Green Acres is a senior citizens' camp, Camp

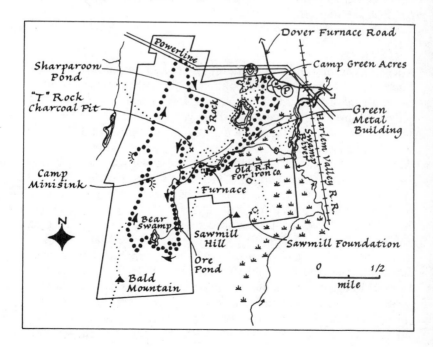

Minisink a youth camp. Both are in full swing during the summer.

Since 1957, Sharparoon has been closed to the public. Helen Lazarides, director for Camp Green Acres, has kindly given permission for the inclusion of Sharparoon in this book. For the first time in a long time, strictly *by appointment only*, and only during fall, winter, and spring, Sharparoon is open to the general public.

ACCESS

From the Wingdale traffic light at the intersection of NY 22 with Dutchess County 21, head north on NY 22, 2.5 miles, to a left turn onto Dutchess County 26 *west*/Dover Furnace Road. Drive 0.5 miles, over two bridges. Watch on the left for a newer building called Zaccara Center. If you come to Camp Green Acres, you've gone one driveway too far. Park at Zaccara Center and register at the office.

Sharparoon is open to the public from Labor Day to Memorial Day by appointment only. The grounds are closed in the summer when the camps are in full operation. Phone: Helen Lazarides' office at Camp Green Acres, (914) 832-6151. Hours are from dawn to dusk. No dogs are allowed.

TRAIL

Arrive in the morning, as you will need about three hours just to reach Bear Swamp. After checking in at the office, walk west along Dover Furnace Road to the white pine forest, where two pillars announce: Camp Sharparoon, and there is a sign for Camp Minisink. The Minisink were the band that became the core group of the historic Munsee Indians. *Munsee* means "person from Minisink." *Minisink* means "on the island." The Esopus, who spoke the same Munsee dialect, later joined the Minisink. The word *Munsee* became more and more popular a reference to both groups until it was applied to all speakers of the Munsee form of the Delaware language. Walk around the pillars and down the road into the impressive pine plantation planted by the Youth Conservation Corps in the 1930s and 1940s.

The steep-sided pit on your left with the swamp at its bottom is an iron mine. The Hudson Highlands, the Fishkill Range, and the South Taconic Range were famous for their iron ore, present in varying purities. (Historically, the name Fishkill Range was applied to the mountains that began at the Hudson River with Breakneck Ridge and ran inland and then north to end with the Harlem Valley's West

Mountain.) Mines begun in colonial times reached their peak operation in the 1880s. Iron companies employed thousands of men as ore-diggers, coal-men, colliers, smelters, teamsters, and limestone-diggers, creating many of our hamlets and towns. When the mines were no longer operating, many of the pits filled with water to become lakes.

Walk down to the beach at Sharparoon Pond for a look, then return to the road and continue through Camp Minisink. At the fork, bear left of the craft porch, then straight across the lawn past volleyball and basketball courts toward a green metal-sided building where you will meet a dirt road. Turn right.

This is the original road that connected the furnace with the hamlet of Dover Furnace in the 1800s. Keep straight, past the yellow "Caution Drive Slowly" sign. Pass another steep-sided mine pit on your right. When the woods open into a field, bear right to the furnace stack.

Built in 1881 at the height of the iron mining industry, the Sharparoon Hot Blast Charcoal Furnace smelted bog iron or limonite ore dug from the Foss Ore Bed, just up the hill. After the ore was washed and crushed, it was stored in warehouses whose foundations you see behind and above the furnace.

The furnace itself is built of white Harlem Valley marble. Its innards are lined with layers of a special fire brick, called "bosh," which is more porous than ordinary brick for greater heat retention. Much of this brick has turned back into sand. On top of this furnace stack sat a tall wooden building, where people worked and where coal and ore were stored, with more buildings all around.

From the warehouses, charcoal was hauled across a bridge to the furnace and dumped directly into the top of the furnace stack. The charcoal was lit, and on top of it was layered limestone, as a flux, and the iron ore.

What is charcoal? Cut down a forest. Dig a pit. Stack twenty-five cords of logs just right. Cover with soil and leaves. Set on fire and let smoulder for about a month, watching like a hawk. Too hot, and the wood burns to ash. Just the right temperature, and the wood carbonizes into what feels like a crumbly rock: charcoal.

Who would do such work? Colliers. Charcoal makers. Men willing to spend days without sleep and months away from the human race, watching their charcoal pits.

Twenty-five cords of wood, or one pit, yielded up to two thousand

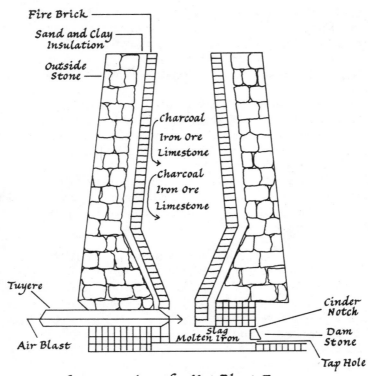

Fire Brick

Sand and Clay Insulation

Outside Stone

Charcoal
Iron Ore
Limestone

Charcoal
Iron Ore
Limestone

Tuyere

Air Blast

Cinder Notch

Slag
Molten Iron

Dam Stone

Tap Hole

Cross-section of a Hot Blast Furnace

(After Jose Alvira)

bushels of charcoal. The Sharparoon Furnace used one thousand bushels of charcoal per *day*. In 1843, within twelve miles of Amenia ten furnaces burned, and more were built later. The appetite for charcoal quickly clear-cut the second and third growth forests of the region. Furnaces for years imported charcoal from Vermont, contributing to the clear-cutting of that state.

With the "charge" of charcoal, limestone, and ore lit and burning in the stack under blasts of hot air, which were funneled through iron pipes up and down the stack, the temperature rose to 2,450 degrees Fahrenheit, the melting point of iron. Carbon from the charcoal combined with oxygen in the iron oxide ore, giving off carbon monoxide, carbon dioxide, and pure molten iron. Impurities melted and combined with the molten limestone to form slag. The charge slowly descended the stack to a hearth at the bottom, the slag floating on top of the iron. The slag was drawn out through the hearth's upper cinder notch. The molten iron was drawn out through the tap hole on the bottom and allowed to run onto the floor of a casting shed at the front of the furnace. This floor was lined with a special sand molded into long ditches called "sows" and, off the sows, little ditches called "pigs." This tough but soft pig iron was of a high quality. It was used to make anchors, musket and pistol barrels, wire, car wheels, cannon, and steel.

Walk the road to the left that leads *around* and *behind* the furnace towards the waterfall. Look for iridescent black slag in the road. The warehouse foundations are built of both alkaline, lowland, white Harlem Valley marble and acidic, upland, grey West Mountain micaschist gneiss. The grey schist contains numerous red garnets, though not of gem quality. Water from the waterfall was piped to cool the working iron parts of the furnace. The iron industry died out at the beginning of the 1900s for several reasons: the discovery of purer iron ore in the Mesabi Range in Minnesota, the lack of wood for charcoal, and the failure of the companies to invest in the newer and more efficient Bessemer smelting process.

Follow the old ore road upstream under hemlocks through a gorgeous ravine. At the fork bear left. A beaver dam at the mouth of Ore Pond keeps the Foss Ore Pit well flooded and a deep turquoise. *Keep on the trail.* There are extremely deep vertical shafts beside this ore pit pond that are only lightly plugged at the top by thin layers of wood debris. Were you to step on one of these barely noticeable pits, you might well fall through.

The trail to Bear Swamp skirts to the right of the pond over rocks on top of a waterfall where the iron companies built a dam to hold back Bear Swamp's stream. The trail is faintly marked with old red paint on the trees. At the pond's south end, a beaver lodge is jammed against the opposite bank. Under late-morning sunlight, the water at this end glows an incredible luminous green similar to glacier-fed lakes. Walk under yellow birch and moosewood (striped maple) to where the faint red path leads uphill to Bear Swamp.

Follow this trail with care as it climbs the mountain. Do not mistake old roads for the trail. Watch for the old red marks, and old and infrequent tin can tops marked with white and red. The vegetation changes to xerophytic chestnut oak and scrub oak, mountain laurel,

The stack of the Sharparoon Hot Blast Charcoal Furnace.

lowbush blueberry, mosses, and reindeer lichens. Through the trees stretch views of the Harlem Valley and East Mountain.

The trail levels. Here grow natural wild white pines. Compare their outspread limbs to the tall thin plumes of the tame plantation white pines at Camp Minisink.

Extensive and impressive are the beaver dams of the east shore of Bear Swamp. Tall and arched, they have flooded the swamp to form a pond. After you explore these dams, you can return back the way you came to the furnace. If you want to make an energetic, full-day hike and you have a good sense of direction, then you can make a wide loop.

The damming activity of the beaver has flooded the trail to Bald Mountain. Follow along the south edge of Bear Swamp. Climb around and over the bedrock outcrop into the fern grove, crossed by numerous beaver trails. None of these are human paths. All have been made by beaver waddling and dragging trees. Each path ends in a dug canal at the water's edge. The old cut stumps in the fern grove you see here are evidence of logging, not beavers.

Keep going through the ferns along the pond past any old logging road tracks until the southwest corner of the pond. Turn north to follow this west pond edge for about thirty feet to a brook that tumbles into the pond. There is a big piece of bedrock here. Turn uphill on a path.

The path becomes an old road that curves uphill and left, then right. There are other old logging roads. Do not take them. Keep on the one that is most distinct. It will become more distinct as you go. Do not take the turnoff to Bald Mountain; there is no longer an observation tower, and the hill is no longer bald.

The road follows the ridgeline of West Mountain. There are views at two points, as marked on the map. Timber rattlesnakes live on the ledges and trailing arbutus blooms in the road. "S" and "T" Rocks also provide views of the Harlem Valley and the Housatonic Hills. The road returns you to the hemlock ravine above the furnace.

There are other trails at Sharparoon to explore. Those that are kept maintained are shown on the map.

9. Mary Flagler Cary Arboretum

Location: Millbrook
Distance: 5 miles; 3 to 4 hours
Owner: The New York Botanical Garden

Melbert and Mary Flagler Cary, heirs to the Standard Oil Company fortune, bought fourteen farms on 1,800 acres in the 1930s. In 1971, the estate became the Cary Arboretum under the care of the New York Botanical Garden and, in 1983, the Institute of Ecosystem Studies was established.

Dr. Gene E. Likens's innovative ecological research at the Hubbard Brook forest in New Hampshire is famous worldwide. It was Dr. Likens who documented the presence of acid rain in North America and who alerted us to its dangers. At Cary Arboretum, he has set up a state-of-the art ecological research station and college. Cary's forests, ponds, streams, fields, soils, and climate are being documented to provide a base line for long-term monitoring. There is ongoing research in aquatic ecology, forest ecology, plant-animal interactions, Lyme disease, wildlife management, microbial ecology, nutrient cycling, chemical ecology, and landscape disturbance and recovery. The Institute also runs many public educational classes and field trips.

As a research facility, the Cary forests and fields are closed to visitors. The perennial garden, greenhouse, and two beautiful but small loop trails along Wappinger's Creek are open to the public. Quiet, mostly level, dirt town roads surround the Arboretum's perimeter. From the Arboretum, you can hike the backroads of the Millbrook hunt country, where more bluebirds live than I've seen in my entire life.

ACCESS

From the Taconic State Parkway, exit onto U.S. 44 east. Go nearly two miles to a left onto NY 44A. Drive 1 mile to the Gifford House on the left, where visitors must park and obtain a free access permit. The office is open for permits Monday through Saturday from 9 AM to 3 PM, Sundays from 1 PM to 3 PM. The grounds are open daily from 9 AM until 4 PM but are closed on public holidays, during deer hunting season, drought, heavy snow, and other extreme environmental conditions. No dogs are allowed. Phone: Institute office at the Gifford House, (914) 677-5343.

TRAIL

Park at the Gifford House and obtain the required but free visitor's pass to the Arboretum. You can also pick up a guide to the Wappinger Trail that explains seasonal natural history and ecology. From the parking lot, walk straight back to the lilac collection and old farm equipment, where the Wappinger Trail begins.

Right off the bat, keep your eyes peeled for bluebirds. They sit on phone wires like hunched old men, a unique silhouette of rounded shoulders. Or you may hear their sweet, soft *cher-wee* call. You can

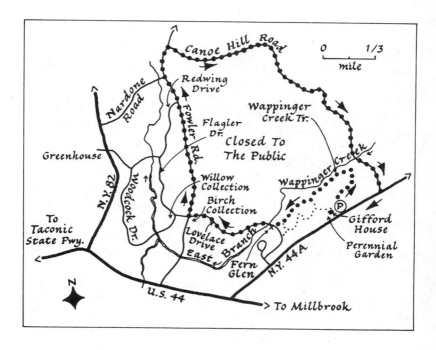

get quite close to them before they fly a short distance off. Our New York State bird with the red breast is blue not because of pigment in its feathers, but because the microscopic structure of its feathers scatters and reflects the light, making it appear a brilliant metallic blue. Pulverize a blue bluebird feather, destroy its structure, and it turns grey. The bluebird, like the robin, is a thrush; the young hatch from pale blue eggs and bear speckled breasts.

Bluebirds were common in the 1800s when the land was mostly fields divided by post-rail fences. Holes in the fence posts were used by bluebirds as nesting sites. Since the forests have grown back and the fence posts have rotted, the bluebird has become rare. Tree holes made by woodpeckers would do, but usually are taken by aggressive starlings, English sparrows, tree swallows, or house wrens.

It has been proven that placing out nesting boxes increases bluebird populations. An entrance hole of less than one and a half inches diameter keeps out starlings, and a location no higher than a fence post discourages English sparrows. The Ralph T. Waterman Bird Club presently maintains thirty-one bluebird boxes in the Cary Arboretum. The Arboretum reports that during the 1988 nesting season 115 young bluebirds were fledged from 123 eggs laid.

The fields and split-rail fences of the Millbrook hunt country are perfect habitat for the bluebird. Watch for them throughout this walk. You may also often hear the loud double squawk or horn-honk of courting male ring-neck pheasants, released by an adjoining sportsmen's club.

The Wappinger Trail loops through a successional field area to the East Branch of Wappinger Creek and what is popularly known as a hemlock cathedral. The word *Wappinger* is the name of the Munsee people who lived in Putnam and Dutchess counties. For years it was believed that *Wappinger* was from the word *wap,* which signifies "dawn," "white," and "east," and from the locative *-ing,* meaning "the place where." In other words, it was thought the Wappinger people were calling themselves "easterners," as did other related Algonquin peoples such as the Abenaki and Wampanoag.

Recent scholarship has shown, however, that *wapingw* is a Munsee Lenape word that means "opossum," literally "white face." Careful readings of earlier chronicles of the Delaware, such as the writings of the Rev. John G. Heckewelder, who lived intimately with the Delaware during the late eighteenth century, reveal that survivors of the Wappinger translated the name as "opossum." It is hard now to know

The Wappinger Creek Trail.

the original meaning of *Wappinger*. The 1683 deed of sale of the Rombout Patent records the original name for Wappinger's Creek: "the Great Wappings Kill, called by the Indians Mawenawasigh."

Turn right onto the Cary Pines Trail through a plantation of white pine and Norway spruce. There is a view of a hemlock ravine. Turn right and go to the paved road, and then right again to follow the paved road. On the way down the hill, you pass all the conifers you just saw on the Wappinger and Cary Pines Trail. Now you can see them without being under them: hemlock, juniper or red cedar, Norway spruce, and white pine. Compare silhouettes, needle colors, and the different way their branches move in a breeze. Once you've learned these characteristics, you can identify these conifers from far away, say, as you stand in a valley looking up at them on a mountain, or from a peak top as you survey the panoramic landscape.

Visit the fern glen, planted with 125 native and exotic fern species. Cross Wappinger Creek. Keep on the paved road. Remember that all internal roads and trails are closed to the public. Go up, around, and down a hill to the white house, which has a birch collection. Our native species are represented, grey, black, yellow, and paper, along with species from around the world. Just beyond is the willow collection. Turn right onto a dirt town road, Flagler Drive. Pass fields, woods, brooks, ponds, marshes, and a handful of private homes. At Nardone Road, keep straight on pavement. Turn right onto the dirt Canoe Hill Road. Return to Gifford House along NY 44A.

10. Buttercup Farm Sanctuary

Location: Stanford
Distance: Variable; 1 to 3 hours
Owner: National Audubon Society

Alastair Martin donated about 550 acres of his farm in parcels to the National Audubon Society during the 1970s and 1980s. Old farm roads and cow paths wind through the pastoral fields, orchards, and forests of the southern parcel of the Sanctuary. On the north side of NY 82, abandoned railroad beds parallel the little brook of Wappinger Creek through a beaver swamp.

ACCESS

For the farm section: the entrance is on NY 82 just south of the intersection with County Route 88. If you are coming from the south, the turn is such an extreme sharp right that it is better to go north to County Route 88, turn around, and approach from the north. Follow the road into the field and park by the locust trees.

For the swamp section: From the farm entrance, go south on NY 82 about 1 mile. Turn right on the one-way road Stissing Lane. Go through the historical hamlet of Stissing. At the stop sign turn right onto Mountain Road. The park entrance will be on your right. Do not block the gate when you park.

No dogs are allowed. For more information, call the sanctuary manager, at (518) 398-5839.

TRAIL

In spring and summer, head straight into the hay fields of tall grasses and find a spot to sit in the sun. See any buttercups? A fitting symbol for this pastoral sanctuary, the buttercup: shining golden in the grasses knee-high up to where the cows once stood. But don't be deceived.

Buttercups are poisonous. The common buttercups of the fields are both European plants: common buttercup (*Ranunculus acris*) and bulbous buttercup (*R. bulbosus*). Have you ever noticed how, if you pick them and get their juice on your hands, your fingers burn? The word "acrid" is derived from the Latin *acris*, which means "sharp." All buttercups, also known as crowfoots, alien and native, contain an acrid irritant poison in their juice, called anemonol or oil of Ranunculus, a combination of anemonin and anemonic acid. In large doses, amenonol causes paralysis, convulsions, then death. Cows who browse in a field of buttercups and eat the pretty, bright things get blisters in their mouths and intestinal tracts. The anemonol passes into their milk, which must be discarded.

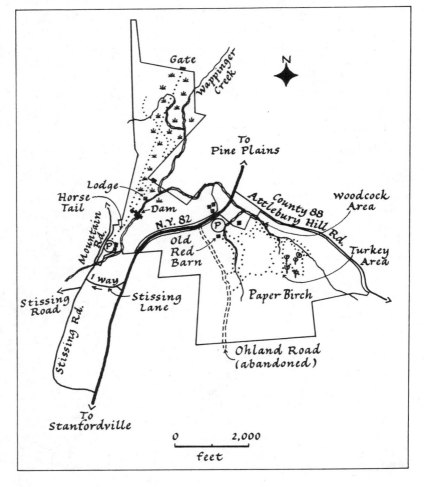

The most poisonous of all is the cursed buttercup (*R. sceleratus*) of swamps. Just two drops of its caustic juice causes fatal inflammation of the alimentary tract. Hippocrates and other ancient Greek physicians used buttercup juice externally to remove leprous nails and tumors. Scribonius Largus described how, "Cunning beggars do use to stampe the leaves and lay it unto their legs and armes, which causeth such filthy ulcers as we daily see (among such wicked vagabondes), to moove the people the more to pittie."

Undeniably, they're pretty, the buttercups. Held close to the chin, the glossy petals reflect yellow light onto any color skin even on an overcast day, regardless of whether or not the chin's owner likes butter.

In these tall-grass fields from April into the summer nest bobolinks and meadowlarks. All our farms would be home to these birds if it weren't for hay mowing. If the first haying is left for after mid-July, the birds can rear their broods in time. But the first haying usually comes some time before, and so there are few ears in the Hudson Valley that hear the musical calls of the bobolink or the meadowlark, the true pastoral songs of summer.

A field of territorial breeding bobolinks and larks is a wonder. The vivacious males fly about just above the grasses singing, perching, fighting, and feeding the young. The air is full with song and sunlight. There, atop a locust, perches a meadowlark, his breast butter-yellow, crossed by a black V, singing full-throated long whistles clearer than the daylight. If you startle him, he spreads his chunky brown wings and skims the field, spreading wide his tail with the outer white feathers, then tilts and drops into the grass.

Atop a slender stem of grass perches a bobolink male in full breeding plumage. He seems like just an ordinary black bird, until he flies and you see he is black only on the breast. On the back of his head shines bright gold, and silver-white crescents deck his back and shoulders. As he flies, he sings, and there is no way to describe it. Imagine sheet metal bent so it twangs. Imagine a robot singing from a bird's throat. Sounds impersonal and metallic? It isn't. It's beautiful.

Both meadowlarks and bobolinks build flimsy grass cups of nests in slight hollows in the ground within the thick cover of the grasses and weeds. During the summer, they pluck insects off the grass stems. Come fall, their diet changes to grass seeds, and they turn into plainer brown birds. The meadowlark flies south to winter in the southern United States, Mexico, Central America, and the West Indies. The

55

The view from Buttercup Farm Sanctuary of Stissing (left) and Little Stissing mountains. The plains of the valley floor once produced most of the milk for New York City.

bobolink undertakes one of the longest migrations of a New World passerine: as much as 5,000 miles south to northern Argentina.

The trails of Buttercup Farm wind through a high diversity of closely packed habitats. There are so many ecotones that birding is excellent throughout the Sanctuary. It is easy enough to find your way along the many paths, not all of which are shown on the map.

If, from the parking area, you choose paths to the left, you will come to a small loop that borders a brook. Mere inches deep, something a child could jump, this book supports trout. Native brook trout need clear, cold, oxygenated water but not much depth. Their bodies are pure muscle. Upstream (in this case, upbrook?) they zoom like torpedoes, noticed usually as only a flash of shadow and a widening V-shaped ripple.

Come on a moonlit spring night to see the woodcock mating dance in the wet bushy field beside this brook. The male woodcock—neckless, chunky, his bill ridiculously long—spirals upward. Wind whistles through his stiff short wings. Trilling, the wind-song warbles louder until in a final burst he plummets, stately and absurd, starlight on his wings and the moon in his eyes, to his mate on the dark moist soil.

The trails wend past stands of sugar maple and hickory, a hill of paper birch and chestnut oak, along clear spring-fed brooks, and through old fields in various stages of succession. In the wet meadows can be found boneset, ladies'-tresses, fringed gentian, and Grass-of-Parnassus. The fruit of the apple orchard is the old barrel variety meant for winter storage. Each apple trunk is riddled with bullet-size holes from yellow-bellied sapsuckers drilling for sap. Throughout Buttercup Farm Sanctuary are serene views of Stissing and Little Stissing Mountains and the Pine Plains valley.

Through the northern swamp section of the Sanctuary flows the mighty Wappinger Creek, at this point but an infant brook. Walk around the gate and down the abandoned railroad bed. Pass on the right the stand of bamboo-like horsetail erect as porcupine needles. Its ancient look-alike ancestor was once forty feet tall. *Equisetum* stems contain large amounts of silica; quartz, a rock of number eight hardness on a scale of one to ten, is made of silica. Without picking them, scratch two horsetail stems together. Hear the silica? Horsetail stems in a colonial housewife's hand could scrub a pot of burnt barley clean in seconds, which led to the plant's other name of scouring rush.

At the intersection the road on the right used to cross Wappinger Creek, but beaver came in the summer of 1988, built their dam, and now all is flooded.

Where's the dam? That long, narrow mess of sticks. The water is slightly higher on the upstream side. At least as of this writing, the dam is a low structure, yet it spans the wetland. Each stick used in the dam's construction has been chewed on both ends. And look at all the chewed tree and bush trunks!

Beaver are rodents big as small dogs. When they take a bite out of a tree trunk, they leave behind big chips of wood. They gnaw off the outer bark to get at the tender, nutritious inner bark of alder, dogwood, birch, willow, and—rare elsewhere but common at this site—elm.

Continue along the railroad bed about fifty feet. On your right out in the swamp is the beavers' lodge, tall as a man. Winter is the best time to go out to it, when the swamp mud is frozen.

Most likely you won't see the beaver themselves. The beaver is a nocturnal species. Your best chance to see one is at dusk if you sit quietly in an inconspicuous manner.

To return to NY 82, follow Mountain Road straight, where it becomes Stissing Road, which loops left to the highway.

11. Thompson Pond Preserve

Location: Pine Plains
Distance: 2.75 miles; 3 to 4 hours
Owner: The Nature Conservancy

Ice stood a mile high and stretched across North America in a blue-white sheet to the North Pole. Then, 10,000 years ago, the Earth warmed. The great glacial sheet melted back but raggedly. Some areas of ice were thicker than others. Some were covered with more rock debris, which temporarily protected the ice from melting. When the glacial sheet melted away, the protected areas of relict ice blocks remained. Outwash streams deposited sand and gravel around and over these blocks. When the ice blocks finally melted, they left steep-sided holes or kettles in the outwash plain.

Perhaps there were several interconnected kettles at Pine Plains that became lakes. Or perhaps there was only one. The kettle in the sand and gravel outwash plain of Pine Plains filled with water and became a lake. Plant growth in protected and shallow areas built up peat muck creating a marsh that separated the lake into three lakes: Twin Island or Mud Lake, Stissing Pond, and Thompson Pond.

ACCESS

From NY 82 just south of Pine Plains, turn west onto Lake Road. Drive 1.5 miles. Dirt pull-off parking is on the left. Phone: office of The Nature Conservancy's Lower Hudson Chapter in Katonah, (914) 232-9431.

TRAIL

The yellow entrance trail to the 466-acre Thompson Pond Preserve leads through black birch woodland bright with sunlight on sedges and hay-scented ferns. The lake lies to the left. Stissing Mountain rises steeply to the right. Groves of ground pine coat the forest floor.

Pass the monument that states, "Thompson Pond, 1973 registered natural landmark, National Park Service." Cross an intermittent stream where witch hazel bushes are growing. Sign your name at the register (be careful of possible wasps in the register box) to help the park committee keep track of use. Such data is highly useful in determining park maintenance and future usage plans. Take the left blue trail for a short loop to the pond shore.

The grey birches and large dead junipers indicate this site was once a field. You can smell the lake ahead on the breeze. Take the left sidetrail for an overlook.

Thompson Pond is a circumneutral bog, which differs from the typical acid northern bogs of New England and Canada. Under Thompson Pond's central open water is a false bottom of soupy peat. Peat is centuries' worth of dead plants, undecayed. Organic material usually decays relatively quickly when there is enough oxygen for the bacteria to work. Therefore the presence of peat usually indicates cold, acid waters with little oxygen present. But the open pond waters of Thompson Pond are neither sterile nor cold, so why is there so much peat? It is thought that the peat was left by an earlier ecosystem, or perhaps is forming only at the margins of the pond—or perhaps both.

Beneath the entire surface of Thompson Pond lies an extensive and deep peat deposit. The pond's vegetation grows by peat rafting. In spring, as the water warms, masses of bottom peat in the central pool are buoyed to the water surface by the gases of decomposition. Most sink come fall, but on many, plants take root: first white water lily, then spikerush and, in one to two years, cattail. The marsh is growing inward toward the deep water on these floating mats. This is happening so slowly, however, that there is no danger of Thompson Pond filling in overnight. Aerial photographs from forty years ago show little change. We are talking geological time here.

Follow the blue loop and rejoin the main yellow trail, turning left. At the fork, go left. There are good views of the pond. Enter dark hemlocks.

The chalk-white paper birches grow larger than any grey birch. Tendrils of thin bark hang loose, brown with stenciled lenticel lines beneath. Follow past the quiet lookout of the knoll and along a steep straight bank that plunges down to the water. You are now walking the original kettle wall. The steep slope is the natural angle of repose of the glacial outwash gravel and sand.

The gravel is buried beneath 10,000 years of soil accumulation. You could easily expose it with a stick. It takes a long time for soil to form, which is why environmentalists get upset when bulldozers negligently scrape it off. For all practical purposes, soil is a nonrenewable resource.

Descend off the wall and follow the edges around a cove. Open water disappears from sight behind a red maple swamp. The trail

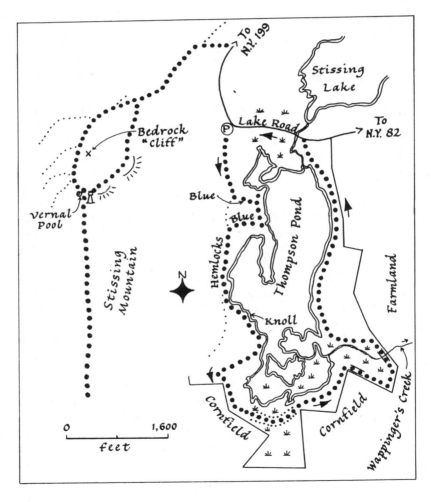

continues on the edge of the kettle bank. The farther you walk from the pond, the older the red maples become.

The trail turns left. Be careful not to mistake a deer trail for this. Keep left past the corn field for the boardwalk through more red maple swamp. On the swamp's other side, the trail heads down to the lake shore. Behind you rises the kettle wall, steep and well-packed from deer visiting the corn fields. Across the pond rises the 1,403-foot-high Precambrian gneiss-granite of Stissing Mountain, an island of the same rock that makes up the Hudson Highlands. Some people theorize that Stissing Mountain got pushed and isolated here 350 million years ago when the North American and African continental plates collided. Such a formation is called a "klippe." Others say it traveled only, perhaps, half a mile, and it was not pushed, but slid downhill from the continent collision, which occurred to the east.

The trail borders farmland. At the second boardwalk you may see the black and white Holsteins beside their barns. Runoff from agricultural operations and lawns sends organic nutrients into water bodies, stimulating plant growth and usually speeding eutrophication. One would need to study Thompson Pond closely to know if such was the case here.

At the third boardwalk, the newborn Wappinger Creek flows out of Thompson Pond. Keep on along the farm edge, then up a knoll to a field. This knoll is just a pile of glacial outwash gravel. Look for places where the gravel is exposed in two-foot-wide circles. These are the nests of snapping turtles whose eggs have been dug up and eaten by raccoons.

The woods look scrubby for a bit, then become mixed sugar maple, black birch, and oak, along with one strange tree. The trail goes uphill slightly, and there's this knobby white oak-like tree with beautiful corrugated bark smack beside the trail. The leaf looks and feels like an elm. It is hop hornbeam (*Ostrya virginiana*), with catkins that fuzz out in spring, and seeds that hang like party decorations. It's one of the heaviest (a cubic foot weighs fifty-one pounds), strongest, and hardest (unsplittable) of timbers.

The trail becomes obscured. Blackberries against the farmer's fence may make the going difficult. Push through (hope you've got on long pants), and you'll pass a scraggly stand of Norway spruce. Now, *that's* the way Norway spruce is supposed to look, like a wild evergreen of the mountains. *That's* what it looks like in its native land. Transplanted to America, Norway spruce takes on a grand and sweeping appearance.

Cattails in the shallows, and white water lilies across the water of Thompson Pond. Stissing Mountain rises in the background.

This is a good example of how a plant species, taken from its native habitat and set loose in a new ecosystem, can change in both appearance and behavior.

At the dirt road turn left. Go down the hill to the boat launch site. You can see much of the shore you walked, and see the different tree communities: red maple swamp and upland forest. Take the trail on the left, past the old dump of china and glass, down the kettle bank, over the stone wall where the trail widens to a dirt road. Turn left at the pavement.

Lake Road cuts through cattails, and one can see that this vast flatland—not just Thompson Pond, but all three ponds—were formed from that one chunk or chunks of glacial ice.

The best way to see this is to climb Stissing Mountain, which contains rocks 1.1 billion years old, the oldest in New York State. There are two ways to do this. A 2.5-mile hike along the crest of the mountain begins 6 miles south at the end of Mountain Road. The steep, short route starts 340 paces north of the Thompson Pond parking pull-off along Lake Road. The trail is on your left, marked near to the ground by a yellow marker. Climb a steep but short slope to an old woods road, where the trail turns left. At the fork farther down the trail, you can go either way. I prefer the right. At each successive intersection, bear left.

At the second fork, a cliff of bedrock juts on your left. Rock tripe lichen grows on the Hudson Highlands gneiss. Examine chunks of gneiss bedrock fallen on the forest floor; see the rust from the magnetic oxide of iron? Same rock we saw at Fahnestock and throughout the Hudson Highlands.

The old fire tower stands not on top, but on Stissing Mountain's north slope. You can climb it to the very top where there stretches a vast panorama, including Thompson Pond, the washout plain, Twin Lake, and Stissing Pond. Imagine that block of ice. Today, the plain is mostly farmland, and a rich aquifer of drinking water. The view stretches to the Catskills and the South Taconics. Atop Stissing Mountain, you can find a few of the scrub oak that are so numerous in the Highlands and Beacons.

The return passes the foundation of the ranger cabin, made of cut blocks of Stissing Mountain gneiss. The trail down is steep, with good views through the trees the entire way.

12. Brace Mountain, Taconic State Park

Location: Millerton
Distance: 7 miles; 6 to 8 hours
Owner: State of New York

Brace Mountain stands 2,311 feet above sea level, the highest mountain in Dutchess County. It is as close as one can come to true wilderness in Dutchess and Putnam counties. Known locally as Monument Mountain because of the cairn on its peak top, Brace is part of the South Taconic Mountains, which continue north through Connecticut, western Massachusetts, and eastern New York into Vermont where they are called the Taconics. Much of this land is protected, so the acreage is large enough to support populations of bobcat and coyote, along with snowshoe hare and occasional visits of black bear. The entire range is actually a klippe, the same as Stissing Mountain, both of which slid into their present locations 450 million years ago during the Taconic Orogeny when North America collided with another continent.

Brace Mountain rises where three states join, and is the divide between the Hudson and Housatonic watersheds. You can climb Brace from New York, Connecticut, or Massachusetts. The views from the top are spectacular, and the vegetation typical of acidic crest tops. The South Taconic Trail in Dutchess County provides short but precipitous access where vibram-soled shoes are a must. Expect snow and ice on the trail until the end of March. The trail is not recommended in winter due to ice. At any time of year expect cold weather.

ACESSS

Take NY 22 north from the traffic light at Millerton for 5.5 miles through the Harlem Valley. Turn right onto Whitehouse Crossing Road. Turn left onto Dutchess County 63/Boston Corners Road. Go 0.25 mile and make a right turn onto Deer Run, into the development,

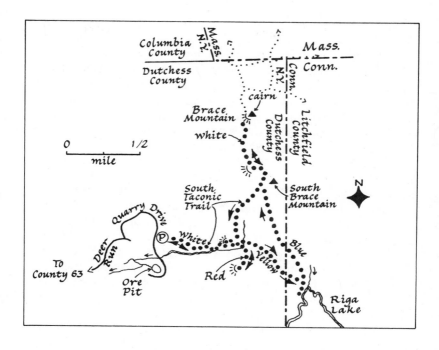

then left onto Quarry Drive. There is South Brace Mountain straight ahead, the hemlock-studded notch to the south our trail. Curve around until you are under the shadow of the hills, where you will see a parking area large enough for two cars on your left. Phone: the Taconic State Park office at Copake Falls, (518) 329-3993.

TRAIL

The white-blazed South Taconic Trail heads east along the edge of a field and into mixed deciduous woods. At the brook, we start to climb. Steep, talus-choked hemlock, paper birch, and striped maple ravines such as this are common along the South Taconic escarpment.

Paper birch (*Betula papyrifera*), the chalk-white tree with the horizontal lenticel lines, can be stripped of its bark in spring when the rising sap makes it slip from the wood with ease, and it is used for many Native American things. (Of course, stripping any tree of its bark kills the tree.) Pliable, it can be sewn with spruce root into various waterproof household containers. The tannin in the bark makes it an excellent bacteria- and fungus-proof wrap for cakes of stored maple sugar, the salt of Native cooking. Buoyant, it can be tied on the ends of fish nets. Canoes, moose-calls, games, toys, and water- and rot-proof wigwam shingles are all made from paper-birch bark. To the Dutchess County rambler, paper birch means The North Country. The middle of Dutchess County is roughly paper birch's southern range limit, a range which extends north to the arctic. Note how most of the paper birches and hemlocks grow only on the opposite side of the ravine on the cooler north-facing slope.

The climb is extremely steep. Take a look at the talus blocks. Rather than the familiar Precambrian Hudson Highlands granite seen on every major hill we've climbed in Dutchess and Putnam counties, we find wavy bands of a Cambrian green-blue metamorphic jumble of schist and phyllite. At the waterfall, the trail turns left and switchbacks along bedrock outcrops where, suddenly, the vegetation changes and we gain our first wide views. The *entire range* of the Catskills and the Harlem Valley lie before us. The abandoned Harlem Railroad, now a long-distance, state-owned trail, runs through the Harlem Valley. You can see Stissing Mountain, with its fire tower on the northern slope. The South Taconics are one of the few places where you can view, in its proper perspective, the true summit of Stissing Mountain. Behind the mountain are the flat-topped Shawangunks. East and north, the rolling Taconic hills (a separate range with the same name) of Columbia County.

At the intersection, turn right for a short side trip to the viewpoint along the red trail. The vegetation is typical South Taconic Highland, xerophytic crestline woodland: stunted chestnut oak, red oak, pitch pine, scrub oak, mountain laurel, lowbush blueberry, reindeer lichens, and sedges. The view at the end is tremendous. South Brace and Alander Mountains shoulder down into the Harlem Valley. Below glints the deep turquoise pool of the quarry for which Quarry Road is named. Turkey vultures glide the thermals *below* us.

Since you've already seen some views, why not visit Riga Lake before continuing up South Brace Mountain? You will not lose any altitude, really, and can ascend South Brace from the west where the grade is far gentler. Return to a few feet before the intersection, duck beneath the hemlocks to where the little waterfall slides down the bedrock outcrop into a pool. Wintergreen grows under the hemlocks, and there are many species of mosses, including much sphagnum. The yellow trail is on the left, in some places painted over red blazes.

Seldom used, this narrow path is wild and remote. It leads along a wetland corridor, then into dense laurel. The convenience of this trail buffers us from the experience of the near-impenetrable mountain laurel habitat. Hikers have no idea what mountain laurel is all about until they must bushwhack through a laurel hell.

At the intersection, turn right on the blue trail. Descend slightly through dense hemlock, mountain laurel, and shining club moss to the northern tip of Riga Lake in the state of Connecticut. Walk out on the beaver dam. What a beautiful, wild-looking place. The beavers flooded the shore, killing some hemlocks. Their barkless trunks, weathered silver, provide valuable nesting holes for woodpeckers.

Return along the blue trail and keep straight for the climb up South Brace Mountain. At the first bedrock outcrop you get a view of Riga Lake, and the Harlem Valley corridor, which disappears into a notch in the hills and curves out of sight. The higher we go, the wider the view—clear south to the Housatonic and Hudson Highlands.

Compare the vegetation here at South Brace with that on top of South Beacon Mountain. Same grasses, sedges, lowbush blueberry, scrub oak, and stunted chestnut oak. The oaks seem sparser, and there are more sedges, but there is one big difference: the addition of stunted paper birch.

The farther north one travels, the less important scrub oak becomes and the greater the paper birch becomes until, walking the arctic-alpine habitats of the end of the Appalachian chain in the Long Range of Newfoundland, one finds only this stunted paper birch before the upright trees totally give way to mats of alpine juniper, arctic birch, crowberry, bearberry, and alpine blueberry. Here at Brace Mountain we see paper birch as it grows in an arctic environment. Three-toothed cinquefoil (*Potentilla tridentata*), an alpine plant familir to those who hike the Presidential Range of the White Mountains in New Hampshire, and bearberry (*Arctostaphylos uva-ursi*), a plant of acidic soils, coastal plains, and the tundra, also grow here at Brace.

Bearberry and three-toothed cinquefoil have long been typical of the Taconics as crevice plants that initiate terrestrial succession on rock. The mountain's past history as pasturage, combined with periodic fires, the harsh climate, and the poor acidic soil have favored a heathlike appearance.

In autumn, these paper birches turn bright yellow. The blueberry turn red. With the sun behind them as it sets over the Catskills, they look on fire, and it is gorgeous up here. As you walk, take care to keep on the trail. These short stubby blueberry bushes cannot survive much trampling.

At the cairn, the trail, now the white South Taconic, heads west to the view of the Catskills, and there is Brace Mountain to the north with the big cairn on top. The trail dips across a saddle where tall trees grow in the deeper, moister soil. This is a dramatic example of how plants depend totally upon soil, climate, and water availability for growth.

From the cairn atop bald Brace Mountain, one views a vast panorama. To the east, the closest hill is Mount Frissell, then, to the right, Round Mountain. To the right of that, the large, bare hill is Bear Mountain, the highest peak in Connecticut. Still to the right but closer is Gridley Mountain. To the north, you can see the long Alander and all the hills of Massachusetts, including the distant but distinctive two-hump profile of 3,491-foot Mount Greylock, one of the highest in the Taconic Range. Down in the Harlem Valley is the town of Copake Falls, Columbia County, where the Harlem Valley Rail-Trail ends. At night, you can see the glow from the lights of Albany. East and south are all the points previously mentioned. The South Taconic Trail continues for some fourteen miles north into Massachusetts to end near Bash Bish Falls. (The New York-New Jersey Trail Conference publishes a topographic map of the trail and region entitled *South Taconic Trails,* trail map fourteen.)

Return south. South or Furnace Pond can be seen behind Riga Lake, the center of the local iron-mining industry that clear-cut the lowland forests for charcoal fuel. Go past the South Brace cairn, descend into stunted oak forest and watch on the right for the white trail. As you descend, note how the steeple-top hemlocks grow only in the notch of the ravine, and how pitch pines grow only on top of the lookout, on the red trail.

New York State Multiple Use Areas

Formerly called state forests, multiple use areas (MUA) are state-owned, mostly forested land where the public can hike, camp, hunt, picnic, cut timber, and, in some places, fish. It's a way for New York State to fulfill some of the numerous and often conflicting taxpayers' outdoor recreational needs while at the same time maintaining environmental quality—the old juggle between use and preservation. Usually, a multiple use area is actively managed for timber production and wildlife habitat. Some MUAs contain trails, often left unmaintained for years.

There are six multiple use areas in Dutchess County. Roeliff Jansen Kill MUA in Milan is undeveloped, which leaves hikers who enjoy the convenience of trails with just five sites in Dutchess County.

Wassaic MUA, 488 acres, located in Wassaic off Tower Hill Road, contains one main dirt road off which branch multitudinous, overgrown woods roads. This is a good place to visit when you want to be alone in the hills with your sketch pad and plant identification books. The four remaining MUAs within Dutchess County are described within the following section of this book.

Putnam County has five multiple use areas, two unique areas, and one wildlife management area. Castle Rock Unique Area is covered

Azalea.

in the Hudson Highlands section of this book. Here is a brief description of those Putnam County MUAs that are largely undeveloped. If you live locally, you might want to visit them.

White Pond MUA, White Pond Road, Kent, 276 acres. A large beautiful lake surrounded by forested hills. One can walk White Pond Road, which is dirt and seldom used by traffic. Open to canoes and rowboats. The boat launch site is by the dam and the parking lot.

Big Buck Mountain MUA, Ressique Road, Kent, 146 acres. A dirt logging road, closed to traffic, climbs the mountain. There are views of the surrounding hills when the leaves are down. Selective timber cutting is ongoing.

California Hill MUA, California Hill Road, Kent, 296 acres. A dirt road closed to traffic, called Mungers Road, leads up the ridge from Peekskill Hollow to an abandoned farm. Numerous wild grapes line the road.

Pudding Street MUA, Pudding Street, Putnam Valley, 74 acres. Extensive logging is ongoing, but the lake is beautiful.

As you can see, there are a few dirt roads to walk, but otherwise these MUAs are bushwhacking country.

So, a total of eight MUA sites in Dutchess and Putnam have trails to hike. These are mostly old farmlands that have succeeded to old fields and upland forests. Compared to other public parks, these lands are empty of visitors. Of course, during autumn hunting season, it's a different story; the MUAs are crawling and, while some think wearing a fluorescent red body suit is protection enough, it is best for the hiker to keep away.

All the multiple use areas are under the jurisdiction of the New York State Department of Environmental Conservation, Forest Service Resource Management Office, which is headquartered at Stony Kill Farm in Wappingers Falls. Their phone number is (914) 831-8780.

Cranberry Mountain Wildlife Management Area and Bog Brook Unique Area, which are included in this section, are administered by the New York State Department of Environmental Conservation, Bureau of Wildlife in New Paltz. Their phone number is (914) 255-5453.

13. Ninham Mountain

Location: Carmel
Distance: 1.5 miles; 2 hours
Owner: State of New York

The 1,023-acre Ninham Mountain MUA is bisected by Gypsy Trail Road. The east side, an old farm in the Pine Pond valley, contains two north-south trails that pass through old fields, deciduous woods, a pond, and plantations of Norway spruce, balsam fir, European larch, and red pine. The west side, the mountain itself, also was farmed, mostly by members of the Smalley family, which is why on old maps the mountain is called Smalleys Hill.

It is a short walk to the 1930s Civilian Conservation Corps (CCC) fire tower atop Ninham Mountain. The 360-degree view shows endless hills forest-cloaked from the Catskills to New York City. The climb up South Beacon Mountain, Anthony's Nose, Sugarloaf, Brace, or Stissing mountains is strenuous; but most everyone can stroll to the top of Ninham Mountain. *Note:* The first set of stairs on the fire tower is missing.

ACCESS

From the village of Carmel, turn west onto NY 301. Cross the West Branch Reservoir causeway, at the end of which take an immediate sharp right onto Gypsy Trail Road/Putnam County 41. Drive two miles, past the first two state forest and forest ranger signs to the third sign. Turn left onto dirt Ninham Mountain Road. Drive uphill to the gate. Do not block the gate or the road when you park. Bring your binoculars.

TRAIL

The gate on the left closes off old Coles Mills Road, which you can hike clear down to NY 301. You want the gate on the right, the one that leads uphill.

Already you have a view of the nearest hills. The road climbs past

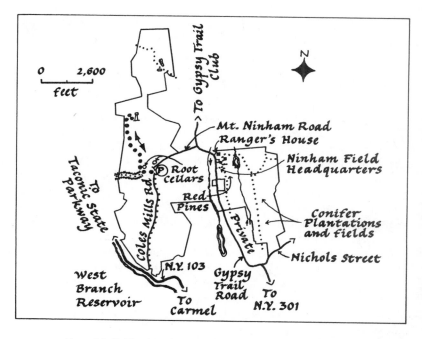

0 2,600
feet

To Gypsy Trail Club

N

To Taconic State Parkway

Mt. Ninham Road
Ranger's House

Ninham Field
Headquarters

Coles Mills Rd.

Root
Cellars

Red
Pines

Private

Conifer
Plantations
and Fields

Nichols Street

West
Branch
Reservoir

N.Y. 103

Gypsy
Trail
Road

To
Carmel

To
N.Y. 301

stone walls, old fields, ancient apple trees, and new stands of sugar maple, ash, black birch, and oak. You can botanize as you go: milk-weed, goldenrods, woodland ferns, lowbush blueberry, sweetfern, and spirea. It's a pleasant climb past all our common native trees. There is black cherry, tulip, red maple, shagbark hickory, witch hazel and sassafras. There are even the common vines: poison ivy, Virginia creeper, and wild grape.

At the top, the road loops past the boarded-up cabins the forest rangers use to a building with no windows and a locked door. From inside comes a buzz. In this building are the radios that relay all the communications for the region: fire, police, civil defense, and ambu-lance.

Leave Ninham Forest's herbaceous plant layer—the niche of oven-bird, towhee, and robin—with the first two steps up the fire tower. Climb to the first landing. You are above the shrub layer, the niche of sparrows. Keep climbing, up through the trunks of the understory, the niche of squirrels and woodpeckers. Toward the top, you emerge above the canopy layer, the tops of the trees spread out in the full sunlight, the niche of eastern oriole and certain butterflies. Each of these forest layers is distinct. Some animal species are adapted to living in only one layer and are seldom seen in the others. Keep climbing to the locked door.

Pine Pond is the larger pond to the east; West Branch Reservoir is the meandering lake. Lake Gleneida sparkles in Carmel. Look at all the open pastures, and the housing that spreads over an entire landscape. There is Interstate 84, and the communications tower on Depot Hill. And the Fahnestock plateau, Bull Hill, and the fire tower on South Beacon Mountain. To the southwest the steepest hills hunch over misty Peekskill Hollow. Power lines march across the hills. The Shawangunks and Catskills loom blue to the west. The wind's terrific up here; the tower moves and vibrates!

Tree canopies form silhouettes that distinguish species: cones of evergreens, red maple swamps at the head of Pine Pond, the dominant oak forest over the rolling rounded hills.

This is the landscape we live on. Running around in our automobiles in the valleys, we seldom get up high enough to see that the majority of the land is hilltop and slope. These endless, low, round summits, once great mountain peaks, were eroded to their roots. Then glacial ice scraped, ground, plucked, and gouged the eroded roots. When the glacier receded, it dumped till and rock debris that became the parent material for our soil and the basins for our lakes, ponds, and swamps. Exfoliation and homogenous weathering further rounded the hills, while streams cut V-shaped valleys.

This was Sachem Daniel Ninham's land, his people's land, Wappinger land. Old papers of the day record the spelling as "Nimham." Ninham was a chief, a sachem. There was no king who presided over *all* the Delaware Indians; traditionally, each village functioned independently. Europeans couldn't understand this. *Each* village had a "king." Equally strange to Europeans was that these village "kings" moved "by the breath of their people." *Loop-way-ee-NOO-ik*, a group of elders, served as advisors to the chief. In wartime, the regular chief stepped down from his role and a war chief skilled in fighting assumed command.

In 1756, various New England and lower-New York tribes joined a large group of Wappinger Munsee led by Daniel Ninham. These Algonquian peoples were refugees, disoriented by the loss of their land and their identity. Their families had been destroyed by smallpox, influenza, and other dread European diseases. The game that their way of life depended upon was gone from the shrinking forests. Their

74

religion, the core of their being, was in a shambles. They had gone off to fight with the British in the French and Indian War only to find, upon their return, that their lands were occupied by the English. No matter where they tried to stay, Europeans kept pressuring them away. They were refugees in every sense of the word. Believing that perhaps the white man's religion would offer them comfort, they even converted to Christianity.

Taking in the view from the fire tower on top of Ninham Mountain.

Ninham's refugee camp moved to the Housatonic Valley, then to Stockbridge, Massachusetts, where it established its church. King Ninham tried for years to regain the land you see from this fire tower. He filed suit in New York State courts, and clearly established that Adolph Philipse obtained his patent five years *before* he made his purchase of a *small* portion of Putnam County. European laws clearly stated that one must first show proof of sale before a patent could be obtained. Furthermore, Ninham established that Philipse gained the rest of today's Putnam County by outright land squatting, with no purchase whatsoever. Despite the evidence, the jury was biased and Ninham lost the suit. Ninham next made the unprecedented and difficult long journey to England to plead that his people be given back their stolen and defrauded lands. He was favorably received in London, given hearings and, with many promises, he returned to Stockbridge with high hopes.

The Revolutionary War made any British promises worthless. Ninham and his men joined the rebels under Ethan Allen, and fought in New York, Pennsylvania, and New Jersey against the British and the Iroquois. Sachem Ninham earned the rank of captain in the American Continental Army. On August 30 and 31, 1778, in one of the fiercest battles of the revolution, Ninham's men and a company of Americans met British troops outside what today is Yonkers. When the Battle of Tibbet's Brook was done, Ninham, his son, and forty Native soldiers were dead. They were buried where they fell in a place now known as Indian Field.

The entire Stockbridge community, into which Ninham's people had been absorbed, was forced to leave because of land pressure from Europeans who now called themselves Americans. Valley by valley they were pushed west to Wisconsin, where some of them remain today. Others ended up in Ontario and Oklahoma. The Stockbridge people today are much intermarried with other Indian tribes and black and white people, and their culture has vanished.

Within the triangle of grass at the intersection of NY 52 and NY 82, in Brinckerhoff near Fishkill, is a monument to the memory of Daniel Ninham erected by New York State in 1937, and Smalleys Hill was renamed Ninham Mountain.

14. Bog Brook

Location: Patterson
Distance: Less than 1 mile; 1 to 2 hours
Owner: State of New York

Imagine a land of raised-ranch houses beside an active beaver pond. Such is Bog Brook Unique Area. *Unique* describes this place well. One hundred thirty-one acres of valuable—even crucial—marsh habitat have been preserved from the pressures of the adjoining raised-ranch development (and may they always remain so), accessible even to the handicapped. For heaven's sake, the beaver dam is against the road! The lodge is *right there*. Come after dinner in spring or early summer, and you are guaranteed to see the beaver.

ACCESS

From Brewster, go north on NY 22 about 3.7 miles. At the Mt. Ebo Corporate Park traffic light, turn west/left onto Doansburgh Road. Drive 0.2 mile and turn west/left onto Foggintown Road. Proceed 0.5 mile to the parking area. When on Foggintown Road you crest a hill, you'll have a view of ridges and a valley. That valley is Bog Brook. Pass by the water control structure that maintains the marsh habitat. You'll see the state sign for the parking lot between immense old sugar maple trees. Phone: New York State Department of Environmental Conservation, Fish and Wildlife Division, (914) 255-5453.

TRAIL

Walk back toward NY 22 along Foggintown Road, lined on the left with Japanese barberry (*Berberis thunbergii*). Brush against the ornamental import gone wild, and the thin sharp thorns penetrate even the thickest of jeans. Throughout autumn and winter, you'll find the bright red berries. Scratch a twig and you'll see the bright yellow berberin-containing wood. Barberry roots were used for centuries in Eurasia to dye leather yellow.

At the water control structure (fancy name for a dam), you've an

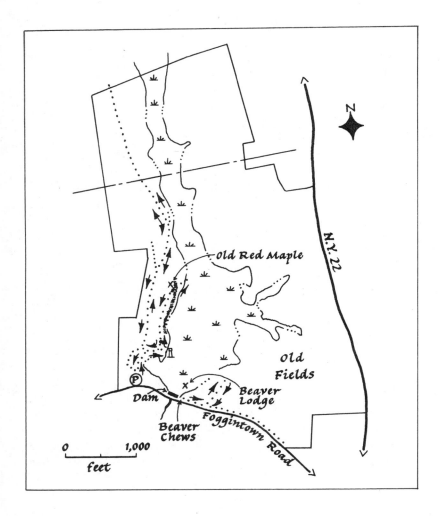

open view of the water and the marsh. Wood duck nesting boxes are placed among the purple loosestrife, phragmites, and cattail. When the leaves are down, it is easy to spot the beaver lodge. On the shore, many saplings and shrubs are chewed to stumps. You can see the beaver's individual teeth marks. The water control structure replaces an old beaver dam and stabilizes the water level of the marsh. But, the sound of water falling is what triggers beaver damming behavior, and the resident beaver are forever plugging the spillway grate with mud. In the past, beaver succeeded in flooding the road, and the state had the rodents trapped out. In 1988, wild beaver returned, probably following the network of streams, brooks, and marshes that web the landscape. Wildlife managers are working with the beaver this time, attempting to keep the water moving and the beaver safe.

These particular beaver seem well-adapted to living beside raised ranches, in public view. They are quite unafraid, especially in the spring. Seat yourself on the concrete and hold still. Better yet, sit on the ground with your back to the concrete. This way you'll blend in rather than be silhouetted against the sky. Around 6:30 P.M. in spring (or at dusk) the beaver emerge from the lodge. Only their heads and hindquarters breach the water as they swim. When they spot you, which they will, they'll give an alarm: raise their tail and smack it loudly against the water as they dive. It happens almost too quickly to see, and the splash is big. But beaver *are* big, large as Labrador retrievers, without the height.

After an alarm tail-smack, the beaver may swim off into the marsh to cut saplings or feed. As I sat on the dam one April evening, waiting, a beaver returned with a sapling in its mouth, swam right up to the dam at my feet, dove, affixed the sapling underwater, and resurfaced. With what greater ease can one observe wildlife?

While you're waiting for the beaver to reappear, there are plenty of other animals to watch. Swallows swoop over the marsh feeding, red-winged blackbirds and grackles smack and trill, showy wood ducks and Canada geese wing overhead, land, take off. Turtles sun on the banks. Diving beetles and crayfish swim in the water. The marsh bustles and teems.

Back in the loosestrife and sedges the hordes of spring peepers begin to sing in April. No larger than a man's fingernail, the male tree frogs inflate their throat pouches and force air over their vocal cords in an ear-piercing whistle. I am always amazed that such tiny throats can cause such clamor. You can hear a pond of them a half mile or more away. There can be hundreds of them going at it, all spring long, all day and night, screeching from practically every unpolluted wetland pool and swamp, each male identifying his territory and shrieking for a mate. As spring progresses, the peepers are joined by the quacking of the wood frog, then the trilling of the American toad, and then the bleating of the Fowler's toad.

If you want to do some walking, on the east side of the dam a trail turns left and runs for a short distance along the field/swamp ecotone past speckled alder, crab apple, red cedar, multi-flora rose, red-osier dogwood, willows, and black cherry.

Another trail beside Foggintown Road continues uphill. Bog Brook's property extends to NY 22. A working dairy cow farm until the early 1960s, the pastures are at the early successional stage, still grassy but getting overgrown with goldenrod and dogwood. Deer trails run in all directions. You can push through the grasses and follow the deer paths to your heart's content. Some lead uphill, some down to the marsh and through it. Fun at any time of the year, the trails are best when the leaves are down; then the abrupt boundaries between marsh and dry field are simple to see. This is an enjoyable thing, to be able to see at a glance the soil types and their corresponding plant communities across the landscape.

To explore the west side of the marsh, follow the trail from the parking lot into the woods. You'll come to a brown metal box on a pole. Inside is a self-guided booklet. Take one and proceed down the right fork.

At post number six, keep right through the stone wall for the observation tower. The view is through the bushes. Return to the trail and turn right. Keep an eye out for trees felled by beaver. At the smooth sumac, take the narrow trail on the right. Just before the path crosses a stone wall, it passes between a clump of muscled ironwood trees.

The trail follows a stone wall along the marsh edge. Stone walls were a common technique used by early farmers to keep their livestock out of the mud while at the same time clearing the land of glacial cobbles. Nearly every marsh in Putnam and Dutchess counties has a stone wall that separates it from what was once field and is now new forest. This shows you how extensively the area was farmed. These stone walls follow the narrow ecotone line between the two habitats.

There are good glimpses of the marsh. In August, the bright purple loosestrife blooms, beloved by bees. Joe-Pye weed is the shaggier, pinker bloom.

Eupatorium purpureum belongs to a genus with members throughout the world renowed for their medicinal virtues, especially for curing cholera, typhus, typhoid, smallpox, and various fevers, and as an antidote to the poisonous bites or stings of reptiles and insects. In New England, the story is told of Joe-Pye, or Jopi, a Native American healer who traveled the land curing whites and Indians alike of the terrible and much-feared typhus fever through the use of this plant that now bears his name. Joe-Pye weed was an official drug in the *U.S. Pharmacopeia* from 1820 to 1842, at a time when herbal medicine was still honored.

Perhaps the most prevalent plant in the marsh is purple loosestrife (*Lythrum salicaria*). Hudsonia, Ltd., the ecological research group based at Bard College in Annandale, reports that purple loosestrife, an alien plant, outcompetes native cattails, sedges, and bulrushes. Yet, they have also found that loosestrife has become an important food source for cecropia moth caterpillars, and that American goldfinches nest in it. Undeniably, loosestrife is pretty, and so familiar to Americans that in Peterson's wildflower guide it rates a color plate.

Where the path crosses the stone wall that parallels the marsh, a red maple stands. Poison ivy curls up it, and its heart is rotted. Yet, incredibly, the thing's alive. The heart of any live tree, its heartwood, is dead. Like a bone, the heartwood holds up the tree. Should moisture enter through a crack or a wound in the bark, the heartwood can rot, but the tree need not die. So long as the green cambium layer beneath the inner bark remains intact from root to branch—even for mere inches—the tree will live. Of course, the tree is not healthy, and eventually will fall down, if nothing else.

The path passes tussock sedge hummocks and cinnamon fern to end at a stream channel. In winter, you can explore further, being sure to test any ice on which you intend to step. In spring, search for peepers. They'll know you're coming, and will fall silent. Walk up to the water's edge and stand absolutely still. In minutes, they'll resume their chorus. Most peepers sing from beneath the shelter of an overhang of sedge and are invisible. But every so often, one swims in the open water. Should you catch one (a difficult thing), you'll see a tiny brown tree frog with a "suction cup" on the end of each toe and a brown *X* across its back, which gives the peeper its scientific name: *Hyla crucifer*, or "cross-bearer." You would need a microscope to see the bristles on the toe pads that allow the frog to climb trees and even walk up glass. Release the peeper back to the swamp. Come early summer, the peepers disperse into the woods and meadows and are rarely seen.

On the return, if you wish to walk farther, at post number six bear right uphill and right again at number eleven. This narrow trail continues on past stone walls and open woods, getting thinner and more obscure until it seems little better than a game trail. Test your woods-walking skills; how far can you follow the trail up Bog Brook Valley?

15. Cranberry Mountain

Location: Patterson
Distance: 3.3 miles; 2 to 3 hours
Owner: State of New York

Cranberry Mountain contains 464 acres of forest, field, and wetland habitats managed to produce wildlife. There are bluebird and wood duck nesting boxes, cuttings, plantings, water impoundments, and hedgerows; those good things that encourage ecotones and vigorous sapling growth for wildlife cover, food, and reproduction sites. Hunting and fishing are popular pastimes at Cranberry Mountain, along with hiking.

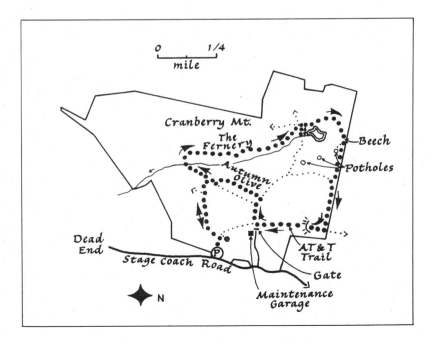

ACCESS

Just south (0.3 miles) of the intersection of NY 311 and NY 22, turn east onto Birch Hill Road. If you are coming north on NY 22, use Old Route 22 to lead you to Birch Hill Road. Drive behind Birch Hill Inn, past Big Birch ski area, and on for 2.6 miles to the T intersection. Turn right onto Stage Coach Road. Go 0.7 miles. Don't worry as the road narrows. It will turn to dirt. Go 0.1 mile further. The parking entrance is on the right.

TRAIL

Pick a bright, breezy summer's day; the woods look best then. From the parking area, squeeze between the boulders and head on out.

Most of Cranberry Mountain's trails are forest roads, some newly cut, others well established, some left to be reclaimed by the forest. Many are overgrown with tall brambles and weeds (which shows you how much the park gets used—hardly at all). You'll want to wear long pants when you come here.

Follow the road. It's wide enough to function as an ecotone strip of field and grows many of the region's alien and native field species. An ecotone is any place where two plant communities meet, the species of each intermingling. Ecotones are the favorite habitat of much wildlife and many birds, especially since most need a combination of habitats to complete their life histories. Wildlife managers manage for ecotones. The border between a field and a forest is an ecotone, as is the border between a marsh and a field, or a tidal cove and a forest.

Near the top of the hill, take your first left. The summer sun falls through the oaks and red maples (a combination found throughout Cranberry Mountain) onto ferns, blueberries both high and lowbush, meadowsweet, and sweet fern. The peculiar waxy-dry-sweet-warm smell of a xeric upland forest wafts through the air.

At the intersection, turn left downhill through bright young woods sunny and scented with groves of woodland ferns. At the bottom of the hill is a swampy red maple forest supported by the moisture from an intermittent stream. Cross the brook and follow upstream. You are walking along the foot of Cranberry Mountain. Notice the difference in forests on either side of the trail: to your right, the dark green of swamp; to the left, the brighter green of upland forest. The trail follows the ecotone line where the plant communities change abruptly due to a change in soil moisture.

The swamp is really just a bottomland growth of red maple and cinnamon fern. In April, the red maples bloom. The stocky deep red blooms with two thread-like pistil parts are females. The red and yellow ones are males, their fuzzy parts the pollen-bearing anthers. Usually, red maple trees are either male or female. Occasionally, they're both, half the tree male, half female. The male pollen fertilizes the female eggs, and from her two pistils grow the twin wings of poly-noses, or samaras, a seed inside each.

The trail gradually climbs uphill. Enter the fernery. The foot of Cranberry Mountain grows profuse beds of New York, hayscented, lowland lady, bracken, and cinnamon ferns. Exposed in the trail are the rootstocks or rhizomes: fibrous black hairy things in mounds. Between the ferns grow club mosses: shining club moss, princess pine (looks like a miniature pine tree), and ground pine. These are protected plants, some of them rare. The spores gathered from the candelabra stalks of *lycopodium* are flammable. During the Revolutionary War, they were used as gunpowder.

Keep straight on the main trail until the intersection with another woods road. Turn right, then left for a sidetrip to the pond, which is man-made, as are all the ponds at Cranberry Mountain. You can tell in August how many resident ducks are molting by the amount of feather flotsam on the water. Swallows hunt in the air and ducks preen on the logs. Stocked bass splash in the shallows flailing after smaller fish.

Return, bearing right, and turn right to continue. Have you noticed small frogs leaping out of your way? These are young pickerel frogs. Not all frogs live in ponds. A great number of species forage in the woods where it's moist enough to keep their skins supple.

Watch the trail for turkey feathers. Turkey are wary fowl, so you probably won't see the birds themselves. August is a good time to find their large flat-tipped molted plumes. Turkey used to be one of the most important birds of the eastern woodland biome, part of the chestnut-turkey-oak-deer-hickory-black bear complex. Turkey and deer subsisted off chestnuts, and the American chestnut dominated the upland forests of the Hudson Valley. In 1904, Asiatic chestnuts were introduced to New York City. These had always been the natural host of a fungus disease that did not kill them, but it wiped out the American chestnut. Such habitat destruction, in addition to uncontrolled commercial hunting and the lack of protective laws, also wiped out the turkey and the deer. Over the years, oaks filled the niche that once belonged to chestnuts and became the new dominant tree of the region. Some people think ruffed grouse partially moved into the turkey's former position. Under heavy legal protection, white-tailed deer were reintroduced from midwestern stock. When wild turkey wandered back into New York State from Pennsylvania in the 1940s, they were adapted to subsisting off acorns, rather than chestnuts and acorns. With the help of the State Conservation Department, turkey

The fernery.

are now found throughout New York. The turkey of Cranberry Mountain probably wandered in from the Taconics where they had been reintroduced.

The trail climbs to upland forest. When it levels and begins to turn right, on the left will be a clump of ghost-pale beech. Opposite them grow chestnut oak with deep-clefted bark. Chestnut oak leaves look similar to American chestnut leaves.

If you've had enough, there are a number of ways back from here. If you're in for the entire tour, then take the trail on the left and head uphill. It's a climb, but the higher you go, the more hills you'll see through the trees. The view is best in winter, but nice in summer, too. The trees live in harsh xeric conditions, and their stunted short size reflects this.

At AT&T's trans-Atlantic cable right-of-way, turn right. Here is the best view. Nothing spectacular, but the blue hills and the distance are enjoyable. It's all downhill from here.

At the intersection, turn right. These fields, kept from succeeding to brush and forest by biannual mowing, are overgrown with native and alien wildflowers. Each species flowers and reproduces at its most advantageous time. Among them, hawkweed and milkweed are early summer blooms. They are followed by campian and ox-eye daisy, then Queen-Anne's lace, black-eyed Susan, thistle, chicory, and, finally, goldenrod.

Sixty-nine species of goldenrod (*Solidago*) grow in the northeast. Goldenrod pollen is so heavy it can not be lifted by winds, so none of those sixty–nine species causes hay fever unless you walk right through it. It is ragweed that does that. In August, how many different types of goldenrod can you find in this field? At first glance, it's all just yellow flowers. Look closer, and here is one with sprays arranged like a trumpet, here's another with stars of blossoms along one central stalk, and another flat as a table top.

Go to the third field. There stands the long ridge of Cranberry Mountain before you. Turkey vultures soar the thermals. At the autumn olive hedgerow on the left, turn left into the twin tire marks of the trail. This may be hard to see. Follow the autumn olive, an oriental silverberry planted in the 1960s to provide food and cover for birds and rabbit.

Enter cool woods. Turn right, then left, to return to the parking lot.

16. Depot Hill

Location: Beekman
Distance: 1.5 miles; 2 hours
Owner: State of New York

Named for a railroad station that once sheltered passengers and freight at the foot of the ridge, Depot Hill is actually one small section of a nearly continuous ridge, historically called the Fishkill Range, which runs from Breakneck Ridge east to the Harlem Valley. Geologically, it is all the same Hudson Highlands gneiss and granite. This bedrock underlies the shallow soil of Depot Hill so near to the soil surface that in every ravine and hollow rainwater gets trapped and held. It is pleasant to walk in a forest of upland trees adjacent to thickets of swamp azalea. The bedrock pokes up in numerous outcrops covered with rock tripe. And, in winter, there's the springtails.

ACCESS

From the intersection of Dutchess County 7 and NY 216 in Poughquag, take NY 216 west 0.6 miles to a left turn onto Depot Hill Road. Follow Depot Hill Road for 2 miles. Park on the left in an unmarked, paved lot at the apex of the hill.

TRAIL

Depot Hill Road has been around a long time. A 1798 map of the town of Beekman shows the entire Fishkill Range area as vacant of civilization. But an 1856 map shows Depot Hill Road in its entirety, along with the house of Charles Freeman. But the road is called Negro Hill Road and the entire area is called Freemanville.

Charles Freeman was an African-American, a freed slave. Lee Eaton, Beekman town historian, thinks perhaps Mr. Freeman had recently been freed, and other freed slaves came to join him. Or perhaps he had been a freeman for a while, and recently freed slaves came to live with him in a safe community. Likely, we'll never know.

The community is on the old maps: a double row of houses, close together. But, unlike the single widely-spaced homes of white folks in Beekman, the village homes of Freemanville list no owners' names. The information was excluded from the maps and from most of the historical literature.

New York and New England Railroad built a depot station where Negro Hill Road crossed the tracks in 1912, and the name of the road changed to Depot Hill. Today, the station is gone, but the valley echoes most nights to the rumble of Conrail's long freight trains, and the community of black folks remains.

Walk along Depot Hill Road until it turns to dirt. In about 100 feet the Appalachian Trail, marked in white, crosses Depot Hill Road. Turn left onto this path where the trail tilts down a slope into a hollow. The upland oak woods also grow black birch, red maple, beech, mountain laurel, and lowbush blueberry and huckleberry. Come here in winter when there is snow on the ground. The air temperature matters not, but it must be either sunny or partially sunny. Walk down this slope and

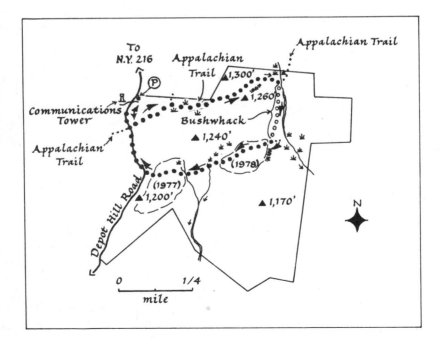

watch the snow for black pepper. Found some? Lean close. Why, the pepper moves! In fact, it springs. You've found springtails!

The snow flea, *Achorutes nivicolus,* lives in soil and leaf litter, under bark, and in decaying wood. It is a scavenger. There can be several million per acre in the soil. Come the winter snows, the springtails crawl through the abundant air space interstices between the snow crystals to the surface. These dead air spaces, by the way, make snow an excellent thermal insulator, dead air being a poor conductor of heat, which is why Eskimos stay warm in snow igloos, and why more woodland plants and burrowing animals survive a winter that has a blanket of snow. To the surface come these springtails, to feed off the algae that grow in the sunlight on top of the snow.

Look at a springtail closely. (I do this by scooping up some snow with a springtail on it.) They are cobalt blue, hairy, with two antennae, a segmented abdomen, and six legs. Their forked tail, or furcula, is kept folded under the abdomen locked in place by a special hook. To jump, the furcula is suddenly set free against the snow, hurling the springtail forward nearly fifteen body lengths. Springtails seem to congregate in footprints, possibly because they can't spring back out once they've sprung in.

Under sunny snow conditions, you can always count on seeing these insects at Depot Hill. There must be billions of them. It's in such wet hollows as this that one finds them. And when you do, "the cold, naked, snow-choked woods"—in the words of the eighteenth century naturalist John Burroughs—become warm and full of life.

The Appalachian Trail passes alongside bedrock outcrops through woods that bloom with shadbush, wild swamp azalea, and mountain laurel. Shadbush (*Amelanchier* sp.) blooms white when the shad flies come out. These are little black flies that emerge to annoyingly cloud around our heads. At this time the shad are running up the Hudson River to spawn. When the shadbush bloomed and the shadflies emerged in the woods, Native Americans knew it was time to move to the shores of the Hudson for the shad harvest.

On the bedrock outcrops grows rock tripe (*Lasallia/Umbilicaria* sp). A family of foliose lichens that grow on acidic rocks, rock tripe looks like limp green-brown leather when wet. When dry, it is brittle. Underneath, it is black. Lichens are extremely sensitive to air pollution, especially sulphur dioxide. There has been a severe decline over the last century in lichen distribution, incidence, and numbers directly attributable to air pollution. We no longer see the spectacular,

The Appalachian Trail through the rocks at Depot Hill Multiple Use Area.

long filamentous lichens draped like hairy beards on our trees, nor cliffs covered in rock tripe. To see the rock tripe profuse on Depot Hill means the air is relatively pure and the area free from vandalism.

Rock tripe is highly susceptible to vandalism. Idle walkers can't seem to resist pulling the "funny scabs" from the rocks. I know of cliffs in certain parks once covered with rock tripe. Over the years the lichens were plucked off, and the cliffs are now barren, and will stay that way. Being a lichen, rock tripe does not easily grow back.

Strange things, lichens are actually two organisms from different kingdoms, a fungus and an alga, living together in harmonious symbiosis. An alga and a fungus took a-lichen to each other, the saying goes. The fungus strands provide the plant structure. The algae spots do the photosynthesizing. The green color of the rock tripe when wet is the color of the algae showing through. When dry, the rock tripe is brown-grey; that's the fungus color.

Total exposure to extreme daily temperature changes, wind, and desiccation present insurmountable growth problems that few plants have solved. A rock tripe specimen begins as a pinhead. One that is a foot across is centuries old. Once established, *lichens* are the ones that sometimes begin the process of terrestrial succession and soil formation. They exude a weak acid against the rock. Dust is trapped beneath them. The thinnest sheet of soil begins to build. Enjoy the rock tripe, but *never* pick it.

The Appalachian Trail crosses a brook, turns left, and soon leaves Depot Hill Multiple Use Area. To make a loop, we will bushwhack. Only attempt this if you have some experience off-trail.

Spicebush marks the brook. In winter, there is no water to see. It is a very small brook. Do not cross it. Turn right and head south downstream. Keep away from the brook itself; you'll only get bogged down in mud. Parallel the brook on high ground. As you go, the brook valley will gradually widen, forcing you to the right. This is okay, so long as you follow the brook south. Stay at the same height and continue. You will intersect a trail, but it may be hard to notice, so stay alert. When you find this trail, turn right.

The trail leads to bedrock outcrops being colonized by lichens and mosses, through woodland burned in 1978, across two brooks to woodland burned in 1977. Note the close-set saplings. Periodic natural fires do not usually destroy forests. They clean out the deadfall and bring vigorous sapling growth in their wake. It is when fires are suppressed by humans for years that deadfall accumulates and the killing inferno of a crown fire eliminates everything. At Depot Hill Road, turn right for the return to the parking area.

17. Taconic–Hereford

Location: Pleasant Valley
Distance: 5.3 miles; 3 hours
Owner: State of New York

If you visit this park in summer, bring your shorts. The soil that underlies Taconic–Hereford MUA is sandy. Once a road is built, it stays a road. Brambles do not overgrow the way they do in other MUAs. (Of course, there are the insects, but by now you've found a repellent that works, yes?)

Taconic–Hereford contains 909 acres of two basic vegetation zones: upland chestnut oak (with some red maple wetland here and there) and the Pond Gut hemlock ravine.

ACCESS

From NY 55 in Freedom Plains, go north on the Taconic State Parkway. The park entrance is just north of Rossway/Drake Road, directly off the northbound lane of the parkway. There is no marked access from the southbound lane.

TRAIL

From the parking lot, take the snowmobile trail that leads north, paralleling the Taconic Parkway for a bit. Chestnut oak (*Quercus prinus*) is the dominant species in a well-drained, rocky soil. Chestnut oak bark is distinctive; the only oak with deep clefts and ridges. The acorns are unique: smooth polished brown, red, and yellow wood shells slippery as marbles.

Should you visit in fall during hunting season, you'll find these acorns. Crack one open with a rock and gingerly take a tiny bite. Yugh! Now hold on, give the thing a chance. Taste that meaty nut flavor? A bit bitter, yes, but, all acorns contain tannic acid. Chestnut oak acorns contain the least.

Acorns are the mainstay of several upland game mammals and birds. They used to be the major wild vegetable component in the diet of

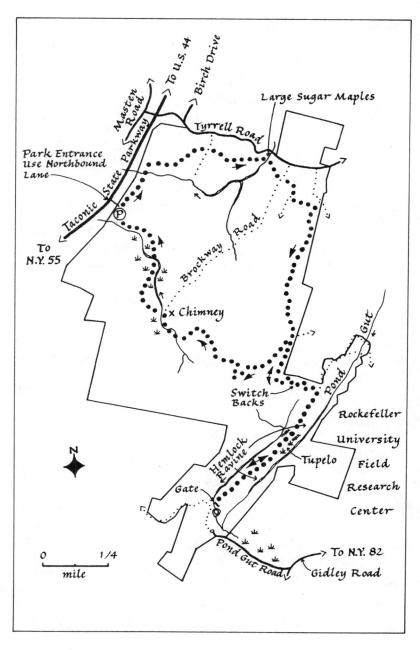

the Native People. If you've fallen in love with the taste of these chestnut oak acorns, take them home. Soak or boil them in a few changes of water to leach out the tannic acid (such stuff is better kept for cures of diarrhea than swallowed into a healthy stomach). Dry your acorns and pound them into flour for acorn nut bread.

Chestnut oak is not alone in the Taconic–Hereford forest. There are red maple, black birch, shagbark and pignut hickory, white ash, black and red oak, occasional white pine and, in lower areas where the soil is moister, sugar maple. Cross a brook where there are several large old sugar maples, our state tree. Atop the dry hills, the woods are nearly pure chestnut oak.

Not a place to visit in a gypsy moth year.

Stay on the snowmobile trail. Cross Brockway Road. Now and then come views of the opposite ridge through the trees.

This word, *taconic*, is a corruption of a native Lenape or Delaware Indian word, originally pronounced *tek-HA-nek*. *Tek* means "cold," and *hane(k)* is "river," so *taconic* in both the Munsee and Unami Lenape dialects means "cold river."

We find ourselves at the top of a chestnut oak hill, faced with switchbacks to the Pond Gut ravine. Down we go. Switchbacks are a technique used to reduce soil erosion on steep slopes. Despite this, the trail is littered with broken slate bedrock exposed by rainfall and trampling. Imagine if the trail plunged straight down? The hill would have ruts yards deep. It is bad form for a hiker to "cut" a switchback, short-cutting straight up or down the slope to save time rather than using the switchback.

Halfway down, hemlock mixes in among the oaks. On the opposite ridge we see an entire slope of hemlock. Notice how the Snowleaf Storm of 1987 damaged the oaks, yet left the hemlocks untouched.

When the trail reaches the junction, the hemlocks turn dense. Thick. Cool. The very air smells moist. Dark it is. The ravine wall plummets downward to Pine Brook far below. The trail turns southwest and follows along at a height. If you've read the Pawling Preserve chapter, you know why the oaks of Taconic–Hereford grow on top of the hills and why the hemlocks grow in the ravine.

Growing in this ravine are plants adapted to the poorly developed, acidic, moist, and densely shaded soil that underlies hemlock forests: pink ladyslipper (*Cypripedium acaule* sp.), rattlesnake plantain orchid (*Goodyera pubescens*), spotted wintergreen (*Chimaphila maculata*), the saprophytic Indian pipe (*Monotropa uniflora*), partridgeberry (*Mitch-*

The old woods road.

ella repens), and mosses. Gone are the club mosses of the dry highland ridges. As with all orchids, the ladyslipper survives through a mutualistic mycorrhizal association between its roots and the soil fungi. Should the orchid be transplanted, the fungi will die, and so also will the ladyslipper.

On the left is a small swamp of red maple, tupelo, and swamp blueberry. See the moss grown over the red maple root hummocks and spread luxuriant over the black water? That's sphagnum. The stuff of which peat moss is made. Stick your fingers into sphagnum—your hand sinks up to the wrist. Pull up one and squeeze. Water runs out as if from a sponge. Sphagnum is absorbent as paper towels. (Actually, it's paper towels that are absorbent as sphagnum.)

Native Peoples and European colonists alike gathered sphagnum, dried it in the sun, and kept it on hand. If they had a wound, they would pad it with sphagnum. Absorbent, it sopped up the blood. Astringent, it stopped the bleeding. Antiseptic, it sped healing. Mar-

95

velous medicine. Historically, sphagnum was used during war when bandages were in short supply. It was also padded beneath babies' bottoms.

The swamp contains a number of other interesting plants: buttonbush and, at its south end, a stand of native swamp loosestrife.

The hemlocks deepen and darken. The land bends into many ravines and hollows. Water rushes in the bottom of the gorge. The forest is nearly pure hemlock. Bushwhack toward the sound of the water and find a place to overlook the gorge and, if you wish, to rest. The ravine bottom and the opposite hill lie within land privately owned by Rockefeller University Field Research Center. Their land in turn surrounds Innisfree Garden. Between the three contiguous properties there are 2,221 acres of valuable wildlife habitat.

The trail veers away from the gorge, the moisture, and the coolness. Black birch and white pine replace the hemlock. The very air smells dryer, warmer, and brighter. Cicadas sing. Oaks appear, and at the gate you are once again in a mixed deciduous forest.

Return back up the ravine trail and reclimb the mountain. When the first switchback levels, watch for a chestnut oak in the center of the trail. Its bark is encrusted with foliose and crustose red, green, gray, black, and blue lichens. As you climb, the chestnut oaks get shorter and more stunted as soil moisture becomes less available. Lowbush blueberry further indicates the dryness of the soil.

At the dirt road junction, turn left. This is another old road, lined with stone walls and cut into the banks. It is mostly downhill from here all the way to your car. The road is wide, the woods open, especially pleasant after that climb. Slowly, the elevation descends and, correspondingly, the soil moisture increases. The forest species composition changes. Chestnut oak give way to white, black, and red oak, then to sugar maple, which are adapted to medium-moist soil. The road passes the brick and stone chimney remains of a house, with one planted Norway spruce behind in the woods. After Brockway Road, our way is lined with ancient sugar maples, encouraged by a previous landowner. You'll pass many sidetrails and roads. Explore them if you wish, or save them for another day.

18. Stissing Mountain

Location: Pine Plains/Stanford
Distance: 2.7 miles; 2 to 3 hours
Owner: State of New York

Stissing Mountain Multiple Use Area straddles the border between Pine Plains and Stanford, and includes a corner of Milan. Half the park's 450 acres is developed with trails. The remainder comprises the southwest slope of Stissing Mountain, and that is bushwhack country. If you would like to climb to the fire tower on top of Stissing Mountain, refer to the Thompson Pond chapter.

ACCESS

From the Taconic State Parkway, go east on NY 199 a short distance to Dutchess County 53. Turn right/south. Go 2.8 miles to Hicks Hill Road. Turn left. The parking pull-off is 0.7 miles down the road on the right.

TRAIL

Our way leads from the parking pull-off through woods that soon open out into a field. Note the junipers, cropped by deer as high up as their lips can reach. Deer cannot subsist on juniper. These ruminants digest their food with the help of bacteria in their stomachs. Research at the Institute of Ecosystem Studies at Cary Arboretum shows that juniper can make up to twenty percent of a deer's total food intake with no ill effect. But when the juniper reaches thirty percent of the total food intake of the deer, the volatile oils in the juniper—the same chemical that repels clothes moths—inhibit the stomach bacteria. A deer with a full stomach of juniper will starve to death.

Stissing Mountain MUA is deer habitat heaven. Once a working farm, the fields have grown into a mosaic of field, shrub, and vigorous young deciduous forest full of tender leafy shoots and buds to browse and dense cover to hide in. What more can a deer ask for? These excellent conditions have led to a large deer population, as indicated by the close-cropped junipers, not a deer's first choice in food.

Giant dragonflies in large numbers zip over the poverty grass and goldenrods, clashing their wings. Poverty grass, or little bluestem grass (*Andropogon virginicus*), has stems colored green, blue, copper, and turquoise. Dragonflies maneuver so expertly that the United States Air Force has for years copied them for jet design. The long abdomen is for balance, and contains no stinger. If you visit after a frost or in early spring, the dragonflies will be absent.

Those occasional giant mounds of fine dirt are ant hills. See all the tunnel openings? Not a place to sit for a rest. Mound-building ants manicure their nest to keep it clear of plants, and thus clear of shade. Any day the sun shines on their mound, warming it, they are active, even in winter.

The trail leads into an upland woods of sugar and red maple, oaks, hickory, and black birch. The Snowleaf Storm of October 1987 damaged these woods heavily. Trees are down. Trees are splintered. Limbs are cracked and fallen. The canopy is half gone. For the first time since this soil supported a pasture, full summer sunlight reaches the forest floor. New growth has been stimulated. New shoots and leaves are flourishing. Likewise are the deer.

At the junction, keep straight. Ahead looms the Precambrian gneiss ridge of Stissing Mountain. Cross the footbridge. If the state has recently mowed, there may be a trail that heads right through the larch grove. Go right if you can. If not, head straight on the dirt road.

Both ways lead past European larch. These deciduous conifers (interesting term) were planted by the state. They, also, received heavy damage from the Snowleaf Storm of 1987. Regrowth has led to strange shapes. Some look like fuzzy cotton swabs. Others are groping octopi. Young larch needles grow singly on the twig. Look at an older branch. The feather-soft needles are arranged in whorls. Come autumn, they turn gold and drop off.

On the old road, pass a red pine stand on your right. The ravine of the brook falls off to your left, steeply. When you come to the young white pine stand on the right, dark and beckoning, watch for any opening, leave the road, and step on into the darkness.

No green plant grows on the needled floor. No needles grow on the pine trunks. The lower pine limbs are dead. Only the tops of the white pines are alive, where the sunlight shines. The circular holes

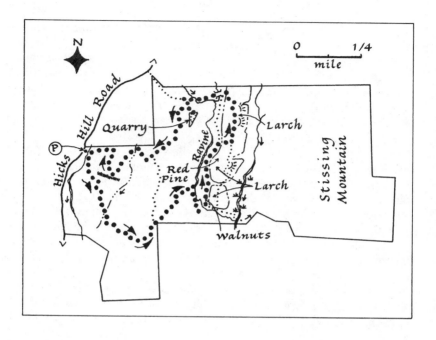

you see are from deer probing their noses into the red needles on the floor for mushrooms.

A yellow trail runs in the center of the grove. Turn left past the white pines in rows, your feet silent on the needles. Emerge into larch. There are views of the hills, a wild north woods look to it all. The place is very quiet, and you're miles and years from civilization. Push through the overgrown parts of the trail. In some spots, Snowleaf bowled over and snapped so many larch that one wonders what tree species will replace them. Take a look at the deciduous seedlings and saplings. Those are the tree species of the next forest for the site, the original inhabitants before the state planted larch in their place.

Just before the next white pine stand, turn left, head downhill, and turn left again to rejoin the dirt road at the ravine brook bridge. Go through the gate and follow the road. Cross a brook. Take the trail on the left, passing through another gate. Keep straight, and you'll come to a pit of gravel dragged from the north 10,000 years ago and dumped by the Wisconsin Glacier. Humans have excavated it and now use it for a shooting range. Young cottonwoods and quaking aspen shimmer on the banks. Backtrack and turn left.

The mosaic of woods, fields, and shrubs appear once again. If you wish to test your trail-sighting skills, watch carefully for the path on the right that heads downhill. If you miss it or don't care for a test, keep straight and you'll come out on the trail on which we began. Turn right and you'll be headed for your car.

All right, here's the test.

Find that right turn-off. There is a yellow arrow in a dead tree, but it's high up and not easy to spot. Head downhill. It's overgrown a bit. Good for deer watching. When you reach a field, just keep in the direction the trail was taking when you last saw it. It'll reappear. There are deer trails here. Don't mistake them for human trails.

In the second field, whorled loosestrife (*Lysimachia quadrifolia*) stipples the clearing. Just beyond the field, *lycopodium* ground pine covers the forest floor. Things start to get difficult. There's no trail. It's more a corridor. Distinguish between the human and the deer trails. At the fork, take the right past the princess pine club moss. In the next field area, head uphill through the field. This one is hard. Look for the opening in the woods that is the yellow trail. If there is no opening, you're following a game trail. The corridor will lead you to the parking lot. If the state has come and newly mown the trail, the thing's a cinch.

19. Lafayetteville

Location: Lafayetteville, Milan
Distance: 2 miles; 2 hours
Owner: State of New York

Lafayetteville MUA is a pretty place. There are no developed trails; most of the 718 acres are accessible only by bushwhacking. But, Wilbur Flats Road, a one-lane dirt track, is seldom used by traffic. It parallels a narrow, deep trout brook past hills of deciduous woods, conifer plantations, wet meadows, and fields. It is a pleasant road to walk for the birder or botanizer. Although one never escapes the sounds of traffic from the Taconic State Parkway or NY 199, there are many wildlife signs to watch for.

ACCESS

From the Taconic State Parkway, exit onto NY 199 east towards Pine Plains. Go about 2 miles, passing the historic hamlet of Lafayetteville and the stagecoach stop at Lafayette House. When Wilbur Pond is on your right, turn left onto Wilbur Flats Road.

TRAIL

Twenty years ago, New York State planted western red pine, Norway spruce, and European larch in the old fields of this preserve. While it is unfortunate that the state spends money to plant unnaturally dense stands of non-native conifers, they have helped to create a close-packed mosaic of upland and wetland ecotones. One can find signs of deer, red fox, cottontail rabbit, ruffed grouse, raccoon, muskrat, and mink. The contrast of the dark conifers against the bright wet meadows and streams is lovely to look at. Still, native species should be preferred to exotics.

Walk down Wilbur Flats Road. Wolf trees grow on your right: old oaks that spread their limbs wide and gobble up the sunlight, left alone in the farmer's field as shade trees. Throughout Lafayetteville are remnants of the farm: posts for split rail fences, corn stalk stubble,

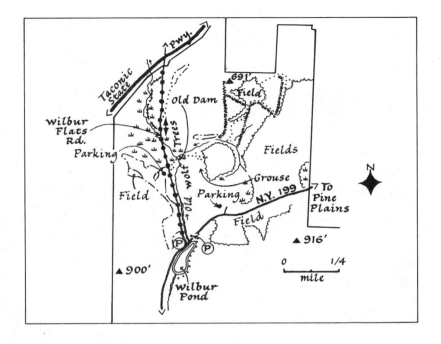

stone walls, and barbed wire (now embedded inside the trees that grew against the wire). Black willow trees line Wilbur Flats Road. Chew on a twig should you have a headache. The entire willow, or *Salix*, genus contains salicin in its inner bark and salicylic acid in its leaves. Willow was used for centuries in Europe and America as a painkiller and febrifuge to cool fever. It is only recently that synthetic acetylsalicylic acid, or aspirin, has supplanted the natural *Salix* species as a medicine.

In the wet meadows and along the road grows sensitive fern. As with ostrich fern, the fertile brown spore-bearing fronds of sensitive fern remain standing throughout the winter to release their spores next spring.

Nearly halfway down Wilbur Flats Road is a parking area on your left. On either side, sportsmen have trampled trails into the woods and fields. These trails may not remain, but as of this writing there is a trail opposite the parking spot. It winds through the young deciduous woods to the brook. The farmer took advantage of a resistant hillock of bedrock and closed up the gap where the brook tumbles, damming the flow and creating a pond. See the stone walls? Eventually, the dam was breached, the pond drained and succeeded to a marsh, then to a wet meadow. We might expect this site to eventually support a red maple stand or, if the soil becomes better drained, a mesic stand of sugar maple, hickory, beech, and oak.

The trail crosses the brook. A yard beyond, watch for a slab of bedrock with a bowl carved into it. Once, this slab was under the current of the brook. Sand was swirled endlessly around and around, slowly scouring out this pothole.

The riparian corridor and ecotone edges of trout brooks like this one provide valuable wildflower cover and habitat for mink, muskrat, racoon, and various birds.

The path leads to an open field on a hill. On your right grow Norway spruce trees (*Picea abies*). Pluck off one needle. Hold the needle by the end where it is attached to the twig and feel the other end on your cheek. Sharp! That's an identifying characteristic of spruce trees: sharp-ended, short, round needles. Hold the needle by its sharp end and bite down on the base, tasting once with the tongue, or until you get a flavor.

Kids say spruce tastes like a Christmas tree. Most evergreens do. Spruce tastes like bubblegum with no sugar, if you can imagine such a thing. And, indeed, until recently, a way to make chewing gum was to slash a spruce tree and let the sap bleed for a week. The sap oozes out to collect into a ball, which the gum harvester cuts off with his knife. Voila! Spruce gum. Stick the ball in your mouth and chew until satisfied. Take it out and keep it in your pocket until next time. It doesn't get used up. I once had a piece of spruce gum for a year, until it finally dropped out of my pocket somewhere and was lost.

If you swallowed the flavor from the base of your spruce needle, you ingested a goodly dose of Vitamin C, manufactured by the spruce tree and stored at the base of its needles. Native Americans chewed native spruce in winter as a way to prevent scurvy.

Beneath the spruces look for blue and white curled droppings and you will have found a grouse roost. You may also find piles of black droppings. These are from one of two animals who passed by. If the droppings are shaped like M & M's, they are from rabbits. If they look more like Milk Duds, they are from deer.

Lafayetteville MUA is the sort of place where you can let your mind turn towards the wild, imagining yourself a deer slipping with stealth along the game trails. Range out into the open field, find the trail that leads across the valley and up into the next, higher field. Explore beneath the dark, dense conifers. Cross the brooks and edge along the marshes. Bushwhack, using deer trails as they suit you. Explore the spots that take your fancy. On the air you may sniff the musky scent of muskrat, the strong odor of mink, or the brief musk of a passing fox. Out of the bushes you may startle grouse, or, rather, they may startle you with a clap and a wing burst. In spring listen for the cock's drumming; sounds like a motorcycle trying to start. Either bushwhack back to Wilbur Flats Road or return along the sportsmen's trail.

You can walk Wilbur Flats Road until the Taconic State Parkway. The return is back the same way.

Millionaires' Row

The aristocratic east bank, the *better bank,* of the Hudson River, is the traditional abode of a landed gentry. With land bought from the Indians, the Livingstons, Van Corlandts, Beekmans, Schuylers, Ten Broecks, Phillipses, and Verplancks were granted their patents by European royalty. These manor lords lived at the expense of their tenants, a feudal serf system that did not end until 1876.

With the onset of the industrial revolution, the scenic east bank experienced another infusion of wealthy estates. The Vanderbilts, Morgans, Tiffanys, Wendels, Rockfellers, Goulds, Reids, and Sterns built mansions along The Gold Coast of the Hudson's shore near their financial empires in New York City.

Just before the twentieth century, Newport and other places became popular. The owners of Millionaires' Row left and their homes were closed. Property prices dropped. Upkeep was too expensive for many of the mansions to remain in private hands. Knowing a good deal when they saw one, tax-exempt medical and religious institutions bought many of the estates, and turned them into monasteries, schools, and hospitals. Others were abandoned. Some were preserved in what today are public parks.

20. Clermont State Historic Site

Location: Germantown
Distance: 3.5 miles; 2 to 3 hours
Owner: State of New York

I know. I know. Germantown is in Columbia County. But thirty-two acres of Clermont State Park do lie in Red Hook, and the place is so close, straddling the county border as it does, that I cannot resist including it in our walks and rambles. So, here it is, another Livingston home.

Robert Livingston, a Scot, acquired 160,000 acres from the Indians. In 1686, Governor Dongan designated it Livingston Manor with Robert Livingston as the Lord. The patent extended for twelve miles

Enjoying the lawns and the ice floes on the Hudson River bluffs of Clermont on a warm spring day.

along the Hudson and east to Massachusetts. In 1728, Livingston's young son, Robert, captured an Indian by the feet as the Native came squirming down the chimney into Robert's bedroom. The Indian was part of a party that had come to murder the family. Impressed, Livingston gave young Robert 13,000 acres of his estate on which to build his home, Clermont.

The Livingstons were a politically important and patriotic family. The British didn't care for them, and in 1777, after sailing through the Great Chain at Anthony's Nose and torching Kingston, they burned Clermont to the ground. Mrs. Margaret Beekman Livingston, wife of Robert Robert Livingston (son of Robert of Clermont) and mother of Robert (later called the Chancellor), immediately rebuilt it. Clermont became state property in 1962. Most visitors come for the view of the river from the house. Few tramp the estate trails that travel through deciduous woods, hemlock stands, and old fields of juniper.

ACCESS

From Tivoli, go north on NY 96. Shortly after crossing the Columbia/Dutchess County line, turn west onto Columbia County Route 6. Follow the signs to Clermont State Historic Site. Park in the parking lot by the house. The mansion is open May 1 through October 31, Wednesday through Sunday, and also for seasonal events. The grounds are open all year from 8 A.M. to sunset. Phone: park office, (518) 537-4240.

TRAIL

From the parking lot, go to the house and stand behind it on the bluff. Across the Hudson is Saugerties and Malden-on-Hudson. Behind these towns stand the blue mountains named Katzberg by the Dutch. Katzberg is roughly translated as "the mountains of lynx and bobcat." Somehow Katzkill, the Dutch name for the stream that flows through the Katzberg, got applied to the entire mountain range. Actually, the Catskills are not mountains, in the sense of being shoved up, as were the Hudson Highlands. They are stream deposits. When the air is clear, you can see the horizontal stripes on some of the Catskill slopes. These were once layers of mud and silt deposited in a sea by rivers that eroded the high mountains to the east. Consolidated

108

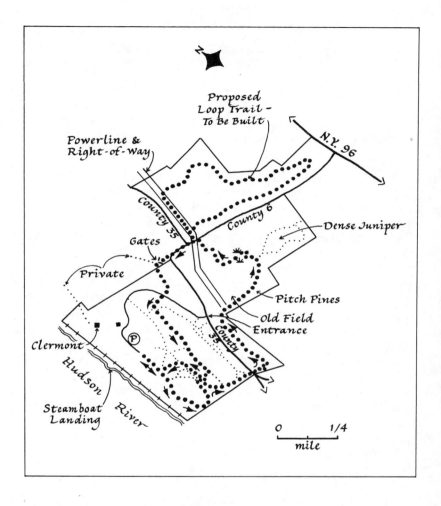

into shales and sandstones, streams eroded valleys to form what we today call the Catskill Mountains.

Following the ridgeline from south to north, there looms Meads Mountain, Overlook Mountain, Indian Head, Plattekill Clove, High Top, Black Dome, Kaaterskill Clove, South Mountain, North Mountain, and Windham High Peak. Masters at acquiring land, the Livingstons came to own all the mountains you are looking at.

Just north, in the middle of the river at low tide can be seen Green

The Catskills From Clermont

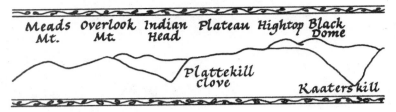

Meads Overlook Indian Plateau Hightop Black
Mt.   Mt.   Head   Dome

Plattekill
clove

Kaaterskill

Flats, a shallow spot of mud and silt that stretches north for a mile. Flats are unstable things, changing year to year from storms, ice movement, shipping, and blind building (for duck hunters). The green stuff of Green Flats is wild-celery (native, important for ducks) and Eurasian water-milfoil (an alien pest that displaces wild-celery). Flats like this are very important feeding and resting habitats for fish (including shad and perhaps sturgeon), turtles, osprey, and waterfowl. Green Flats particularly is a very important resting spot for black and mallard ducks, who may lounge here during the day and fly to Tivoli North Bay to feed at night. All mid-river flats on the Hudson are owned by New York State. In autumn, you'll often see the temporary blinds of duck hunters.

Just south on the west bank and sticking out into the river are—houses? The closest one looks like some kind of grain elevator. That's Saugerties Lighthouse, the oldest lighthouse still standing on the Hudson River. Originally built in 1835, the lightkeeper's house was replaced with a handsome period home in 1869. Starting salary for keepers was $500 a year. They kept their houses spic and span, tended the cut glass lenses, rescued boats and people, and raised their families in isolation. Saugerties Lighthouse was closed in 1954.

South of Saugerties Lighthouse is a long causeway that ends mid-river with a private home. This causeway was the steamship stop Saugerties Landing. Up and down the Hudson River were many landings of the flourishing steamship business. Landing, however, is hardly an appropriate word. On approach, a steamship would cut its engines, slowing enough to allow the captain to throw his passengers and their bags into a rowboat, sprint for the landing, hand them off, throw the next load of passengers and bags in, and row hard for the steamer just as it was coasting out of reach and about to kick its boilers back into full power. Since Chancellor Livingston backed Robert

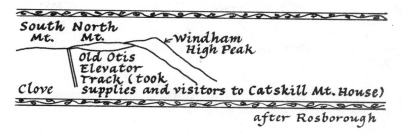

South North
Mt. Mt.

Old Otis
Elevator
Track (took
supplies and visitors to Catskill Mt. House)

Clove

Windham
High Peak

after Rosborough

Fulton's first commercially successful steamship (the *Clermont*), Clermont had its own steamship landing.

There's a lot of history in this view from Clermont, but we are going for a walk.

Return to the parking lot and head south along the bluff top beneath horse chestnut, black walnut, tulip, and locust. The trail begins from the south end of the parking lot as a dirt road. Pass the Arryl House ruins. Keep straight for the white trail, which turns right into the white pine plantation.

There are river views through the typical riverside oak and mixed deciduous woods. The trail loops around past old trees, bedrock outcrops, and tangles of goldenrod and briar. At the stone wall crossing, the annual leaf fall has built up soil atop the stone wall. Plants are sprouting from the top of the wall, and from its sides. The amount of soil formed against and on top of a stone wall is one way to approximate its age. Just beyond the wall, turn right onto the blue trail, and almost immediately right again onto the woods road.

Keep on the road until the first side trail on your right. Take this, and keep straight to a white gate. Cross the paved road diagonally right to pick up the trail. The woods contain all of the trees and shrubs common to valleys of this area: various oaks, black birch, sugar and red maple, hop hornbeam, ironwood, hemlock, shagbark hickory, spicebush, and maple-leaf viburnum. Pass a dark hemlock stand. Listen in winter for birds from the north: juncos, sparrows, and kinglets.

The trail passes into old crop fields overgrown with dogwoods, juniper, and deciduous saplings. Deer trails tramp through the asters and goldenrod, but most herbaceous species have been crowded out by the dogwoods: roundleaf, the familiar flowering, red-panicle, red-osier (the ones with the red stems), and silky dogwoods. All of them have smooth-edged, pointed-tipped, oval leaves whose veins follow along the leaf margins.

Compare the look of these successional fields of native species to the alien multiflora rose, barberry, and bittersweet fields of Bog Brook in Patterson.

Watch on your right for a group of pitch pines (*Pinus rigida*). It was for the pitch in these pines that Queen Anne of England shipped hundreds of poor Palatine Germans to the Hudson Valley. The Palatines denuded the Catskills of their pitch pines, to boil out the tar for Queen Anne's navy. It was these disillusioned Palatines who left their failing tar-making villages to settle Dutchess, Columbia, Orange, and Ulster counties.

At County Route 6, turn left. There are plans to cut a trail through the level successional fields across the road. Check to see if it has been built yet.

To return, walk west on County Route 6. At the curve, continue straight on the dirt road. Stone walls made from the local bedrock line both sides. The right fork leads to Mrs. Honoria Livingston McVitty's home, the last living direct descendant of Chancellor Livingston. Go through the white fence that bars the left fork, and do so carefully. The gates are old. I found that the left gate could be picked up and swung aside, then replaced. Go over the stone wall if you can't get the gate open.

Continue straight at all intersections until you reach "The Inviting Path." When I was a kid, my cousin had a story book with Margaret Prescott Montague's tale of Tony Beaver's logging camp and their Path. There the Path lay, bright and sunny and enticing. Step on it, and who knows where it'd take you. I remember the illustration: big Tony Beaver had stepped on the Path, and it was bucking and smirking as it carried him off.

Well, this is one of those handsome paths: level, carpeted with brown leaves and grass, a border of young trees, a leafy canopy overhead, curving out of sight—a path one could follow all day. Go left at The Inviting Path. Keep on until the blue trail on your right. In winter, stand at this intersection and look at the tilt of the tree trunks. They all lean east, sapling and ancient oak alike, toward grey birches and mature red cedar. Now, what does this mean?

Keep straight on The Inviting Path, now blue, until the blue trail heads downhill. This rejoins the woods road, and you are headed back for the parking lot.

21. Tivoli Bays National Estuarine Research Reserve

Location: Bard College, Annandale
Distance: 4 miles; 3 hours
Owner: State of New York

From Troy north to Lake Tear of the clouds, the Hudson is a river. From Troy south to New York City, it is an estuary. An estuary is a place where fresh water meets salt, and since seas flow inland on the tides, estuaries can be found miles upriver of an ocean. The mixing of salinities, sediments, and organic detritus in an estuary supports an incredibly rich and complex community of plants and animals. Estuaries are special places. But they, along with wetlands, have been considered good dumping grounds for garbage. They have been filled in and used as building sites. Such practices continue today. The National Estuarine Research Reserve System was finally formed in the 1960s to study and preserve these invaluable natural areas.

New York is blessed with an estuary that reaches through the Appalachian Mountains and inland—the lower Hudson River. The Hudson River is one of only seventeen nationwide sites designated as part of the National Estuarine Research Reserve System and consists of 4,000 acres in four sites. Tivoli Bays, 1,468 acres, is one of them.

The glacial gorge of the Hudson riverbed lies below sea level for 152 upstream miles. Tides are felt all the way to Troy, but brackish water only reaches as far north as Poughkeepsie due to the Hudson's tremendous freshwater flow. Therefore, Tivoli Bays are freshwater marshes, the largest undeveloped tidal freshwater wetland complex on the Hudson River. Tivoli North Bay contains an intertidal cattail marsh, tidal creeks, and pools. Shallower South Bay fluxes in a successional stage of mud flat, European water chestnut, spatterdock, arrowhead, and pickerelweed.

Both bays are important feeding, spawning, and nursery areas for Hudson River striped bass, alewife, and blueback herring, especially at the mouths of Stony Creek and the Saw Kill. Along with the usual largemouth and smallmouth bass, white perch, and various minnows, the bays also support the regionally rare American brook lamprey, central mudminnow, and northern hogsucker. There is an extremely large population of snapping turtles in North Tivoli Bay. Many birds breed in the bays, including least and American bitterns, Virginia rail, marsh wren, sora rail, common moorhen, and king rail. Many species of waterfowl use the wetlands during migration times. There are also rare species of plants, such as goldenclub, heartleaf plantain, and Eaton's bur marigold.

ACCESS

Take U.S. 9 to Annandale Road on the Bard College Campus. Turn west onto Cruger Lane. Park in the Cruger Village dormitory lot. Phone: the Hudson River National Estuarine Research Reserve, Bard College Field Station, (914) 758-5193.

TRAIL

Our walk to Cruger Island begins downhill on the dirt road through a successional area of young forest. Pass the white pine stand. At the fork, turn right for a side trip past a tidal black ash, red ash, and red maple swamp to the edge of Tivoli North Bay.

Swamps have trees. Marshes don't. Before you stretches a marsh of acres of pickerel weed, cattail, and arrowhead. Until the late nineteenth century, these bays were open water. The building of the railroad causeways in 1850 cut off the bays from the main channel and allowed the Hudson to flood the new still-water coves twice a day, bringing in sediment and laying it down. Marshes formed, and plants died and decayed. The muck's as deep as twenty-five feet, yet extremely variable. Here it's sand, there it's mud. Should you step into it, you might sink in only six to eight inches—or two to three feet.

Between muck particles are spaces filled with water. The muck is a sponge and holds enormous quantities of fresh water, filtering and purifying it. A ten-acre marsh can hold three million gallons of water. Flood and drinking water protection are two of the special qualities of marsh-fringed estuaries (and all marshes, by the way).

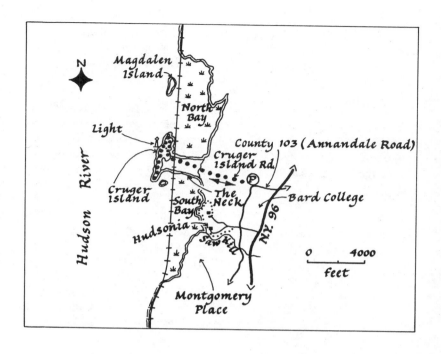

Return to Cruger Road and continue along the man-made causeway built upon what may be a glacial sandspit, or tombolo. If it has been raining, the potholes and ruts in the road will be brimming with water. Search for opossum tracks. The hind foot has a toe dexterous as our thumb, so the footprint resembles a human hand. Swallowtail butterflies sit in pools (that's what you call a collection of butterflies sitting on the ground in the sunlight beside a puddle: a pool).

At one point along the road, the high tide floods from South Bay across into North Bay. It's fun to slosh through, scaring the killifish, but if you don't care to get wet feet, time yourself for low tide. Black, pointed, hard cases, or caltrops, of European water-chestnut from South Bay bob on the current.

Watch for herons, ducks, and other marsh birds. Like Constitution Marsh, this is a spectacular birding spot, heavily used during fall migration. When you arrive at Amtrak's tracks, check for trains and walk north and south along the railroad for a view of North and South Bays.

Return to Cruger Causeway and walk directly across the tracks and slightly right for the trail to Cruger Island. Watch out for trains and don't play chicken. People get killed underestimating the seventy miles per hour speed of an Amtrak cruiser. Approaching trains are surprisingly quiet.

Daylilies and vinca are the remnants of the 1835 estate of John Cruger. Pass the tangle of red maple and mixed deciduous growth to an oak forest adorned with resistant sandstone bedrock outcrops. Come to water, and there's Magdalen Island, part of the reserve, and one of the red railroad bridges that lets water into North Bay. Here grow those strange bushes of the Hudson River shore: indigobush and ninebark.

The trail continues up a slope to the bluff and the view and the waves of the Hudson's main and mighty current, fifty feet deep, ripping past the rocks. Come in winter when the ice is dramatic (if the Causeway isn't blocked with floes). The current in the Hudson rarely exceeds three miles per hour. Yet there is a four-foot rise and fall in the tides, and the flow of the tides dwarfs the river's freshwater output. These tidal fluctuations and currents, plus ship wakes and the frequency of sudden storms, present hazards to small craft and swimmers.

The plants here grow in xeric conditions. Pitch pine, oak, lowbush blueberry, sedges, polypody ferns, and mosses. Northern white cedar grows at the shoreline. At the supreme north tip of the island, the jut of bedrock is coated with blue, orange, green, and grey crustose and foliose lichens. There's a USGS benchmark named and labeled "Lucky." Wonder what that means?

The trail follows south along the edge of the island. Wave erosion has undercut banks and exposed tree roots. There are substantial amounts of poison ivy, so watch your step.

When you reach the shale and sandstone beach and have explored the flotsam, you'll be close to the navigational light and the first view downriver of the Rhinecliff Bridge. There are deep eroded coves here. The trail keeps on for about half a mile. Go as far as you care. The trail ends at a view of South Cruger Island, where John Cruger built ruins to house Yucatan relics. This came during the height of the public craze for sublime scenery and the Hudson River School of romantic painting. To return, come back to the shale beach and watch for the right turnoff through the vinca. Turn right at the next trail and you're on your way home.

Photo by Esther Kiviat

Spatterdock and clouds, late afternoon, Tivoli North Bay, Hudson River National Estuarine Research Reserve.

If you want to learn more about Tivoli Bays and estuaries, visit the Ecology Field Station at the other end of the campus of nearby Bard College on Blithewood Road. The laboratory is shared by the college and Hudsonia Ltd., along with the National Reserve folks. The place is not a public facility, so please do not interrupt researchers from their work. Feel free to look at the exhibits. Leave a note with your name and phone number should you have questions. Hudsonia Ltd. mails an excellent and free newsletter and welcomes donations which support this much needed ecological consulting organization.

22. Montgomery Place

Location: Annandale-on-Hudson
Distance: Less than 1 mile; 1 to 2 hours
Owner: Historic Hudson Valley

Imagine yourself in white evening clothes stepping out onto the veranda. Beyond the lawn and a meadow of wildflowers, the Saw Kill meanders through the still, green marsh of Tivoli South Bay. The Catskills stand high and blue against the sky. A breeze riffles up from the Hudson, blowing the feathery locust tree limbs overhead. It is summer.

As one explores the Hudson Valley, certain family names recur over and over, names of people who held America's purse strings and kept

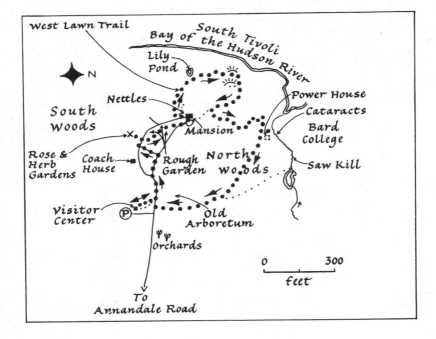

mansions on the Hudson's famous bluffs. Perhaps no name recurs more often than Livingston, whose family members intermarried with other Hudson Valley families to such a degree that Livingston became *the* name of the Hudson Valley.

Montgomery Place was a Livingston home. It is the quintessential summer country house, and its grounds contain the oldest stand of woodlands, it is said, in the Hudson Valley.

ACCESS

From NY 9G in the town of Red Hook, turn west onto Annandale Road/Dutchess County 103. Turn left at the triangle, still Annandale Road. The park's entrance is 0.25 miles on the left.

Montgomery Place is open April to October, daily except for Tuesdays, 10 AM to 5 PM and until sunset on summer weekends. The grounds only are open November, December, and March on weekends only. Montgomery Place is closed January and February. Admission to the grounds costs $3. Include a house tour, and admission comes to $5 for adults, $4.50 seniors, $3 students. Bring a picnic and plan to spend the day. Phone: park office, (914) 758-5461.

TRAIL

Ask for a trail guide at the visitors' center. South Woods, the old growth Montgomery Place hemlock and oak woods, are sensitive to use. To protect them, trails are opened and closed on a rotating basis. Check at the visitors' center to see if they are open. Our described walk is along trails open permanently in North Woods.

Take the trail to the mansion through grounds designed in part by Andrew Jackson Downing. The trail leads to a carriage road and past an English park lawn. Take the left road to the greenhouse and visit the rose and herb garden. Look at the size of the trunks on those native trumpet vines. If you sit patiently, you may see a ruby-throated hummingbird. When you come out under the arched trellis gateway, go straight across the road for the path through the Rough Garden.

Pass the oval reflecting pool beneath hemlocks. Water boatmen, true bugs, oar about under the water using their abnormally long middle legs. They comb the bottom of the pool for plants to suck. When they need oxygen, they surface and trap air bubbles beneath their wings and hairs. Yes, the things have wings, and they can fly, but do so only at night, rocketing out of the water like helium balloons. They can chirp, too.

Go past the urn and along the stone path beside the brook. Many stepping-stone paths branch away from here. Wander away, rejoin the stone path, and follow to the road.

Before you stands the mansion. A double avenue of black locusts ushers the way. Go to the front and proceed to circle the house to the right—such peace and beauty! There are views of the Hudson and the Catskills, and another impressive double row of locusts at the rear. Wallace Bruce, a river writer and historian, gives us a glimpse into

Montgomery Place.

what life must have been like here. In 1818, Mrs. Janet Livingston Montgomery, a widow for fifty years, stood alone on the portico facing the Hudson. The steamship *Richmond* "halted before the mansion; the band played the 'Dead March,' and a salute was fired." Downriver the *Richmond* steamed away bearing the remains of her soldier husband, who had fallen in battle at Quebec, at long last headed for burial in New York City.

Continue on to the West Lawn Trail at the southeast corner of the house. Where the trail begins, there's a dirt road that heads right. Growing on the right of that is a bed of stinging nettles (*Urtica dioica*). Don't touch! The stems are lined with stinging hairs like hypodermic needles, ready to defend against any predatory mouth and just as ready for your bare shin. Should you brush against one, not to worry. Beside the nettles grows curly dock (*Rumex crispus*). Nip a few dock leaves, crush and abrade to extract the juices, and apply. Voila, nettle sting vanishes! Steamed in a pot, nettle stinging hairs are rendered benign, making the young tops an edible spring green.

Do not take the dirt road. Follow instead the trail through the weeds and the meadow. A pond will be on your left, yellow with water lilies in summer. Enter woods at a pair of perfect ship masts of northern white cedars. The deciduous woods change to hemlock as you follow along the river bluff. Some of the red oaks are massive.

The trail breaks out to a view of the bay marsh and the Catskills. The Saw Kill channel, as it slows, bends back on itself in slow meanders through the European water chestnuts of South Tivoli Bay. The trail climbs uphill. Where it levels, a quarry pit was dug on the left. You can hear the cataracts of the Saw Kill in the distance.

The trail to the right dead-ends at the top of the knoll. Stay left, past field garlic and early summer garlic mustard, until the intersection with the Saw Kill Trail. Take it downhill through hemlocks and spicebush into North Woods. The spicebush grows denser as you go down the slope, which corresponds to an increase in soil moisture. Taste a young leaf. Yum! Next time you're baking fish or chicken, wrap the meat in spicebush leaves.

On down to the Saw Kill and a series of fast cataracts and falls. Tivoli South Bay is visible through the trees. The opposite bank is owned by Bard College. Smell something? That's the effluent from the overloaded septic system of Bard College, emptying directly into the Saw Kill just above the cataracts to take advantage of the bubbling, oxygenating action of the waterfalls. Though treated for bacteria, the smell of chlorine and rotten eggs is strong. Even treated, septic effluent is rich in nutrients of which an estuary can assimilate only so much. In summer, the algal bloom at the mouth of the Saw Kill mats two acres or more of South Bay from late July to early October. Secondary sewage treatment plants such as Bard's are the standard throughout the United States. And our country's streams and rivers are the dumping places of worse toxins than sewage. It is sad that we have implemented no better way to dispose of our wastes.

Reach into the Saw Kill (go ahead; it's not poisoned) and pick up a shale slab, turn it over, and search underneath. Anything wiggling? Amazing. Despite the pollution, there are flat stonefly nymphs, round green caddisfly larvae inside pebble houses glued together with their own saliva, and many other aquatic insects that indicate a healthy oxygenated stream. Adult stream-living stoneflies, caddisflies, mayflies, and fishflies are large, lattice-winged creatures. One often sees them clutched onto house screens for no obvious reason, or fluttering around an outdoor light at night. When they mate, the female lays her eggs in the stream. Mayflies do not get to do any laying. The female dies after copulation, falls to the waves and, as she decays, the eggs are released. Mayflies embody that word "ephemeral." Ephemeroptera is their scientific name.

The eggs hatch into nymphs, an aquatic stage between egg and adult. Stream living is dangerous. Let go of your protective rock, and bang! you're downstream and in a fish's mouth. Nymph bodies are designed for life in a place where the current never lets up. They have flat bodies that impede little current, claws to clutch with. And they hardly need to move around. To get food, all they need do is face into the current with open mouth, and let the bits of plant or animal come to them.

When mature, the nymphs climb out of the water. The exoskeletons over their backs crack open. Out emerge the lattice-winged adults. Some of these flies live for months and wing it up all summer. Some stoneflies emerge in winter and can be found crawling on the snow. Some species of the ephemeral mayfly last as adults only one hour. They don't even have mouthparts; one does not eat when there is only one hour for copulation before death.

Keep the nymphs you find safe; put their rock back where it came from.

The trail continues past the shell of the mansion's powerhouse and becomes a dirt road that leads back towards the visitors' center.

23. Ferncliff Forest Game Refuge and Forest Preserve

Location: Rhinebeck
Distance: 2.25 miles; 2 to 3 hours
Owner: Ferncliff Forest, Inc.

Ferncliff is a 192-acre forest in an area in demand for housing. The woods are charming in summer; the mixed deciduous and hemlock stands grow on a folded ravine and knoll landscape.

Ferncliff Forest was part of a 2,800-acre estate amassed by John Jacob Astor, the wealthiest man in the country in the late 1800s. The estate remained in family hands until the 1950s, when it went on the market in parcels. Homer Staley, a local retired businessman who had grown up in the area, hunted and camped in the Ferncliff woods as a boy. In 1963 Staley realized the development pressures being placed on the wood and asked Brooke Russell Astor to save the forest. Astor gave the land as a gift to the Rotary Club of Rhinebeck under a twenty-year conservation easement. When the easement came close to its end, Staley formed a private corporation to keep Ferncliff Forest wild forever. The park is totally dependent on private contributions.

ACCESS

From the village of Rhinebeck, drive north on U.S. 9. Just before Northern Dutchess Hospital, turn left onto Montgomery Street. Drive 0.6 miles. Take the left fork, Mount Rutsen Road. Drive 1.1 miles. The park entrance is on the left, with parking in a pull-off. Additional parking is just beyond on the right in another pull-off. There is also another entrance to Ferncliff on River Road. Homer Staley is Ranger for Ferncliff. His phone is (914) 876-4229. The park is always open.

TRAIL

Walk South Pond Trail to Mount Rutsen Pond. Here is a maintenance shed with a map and information. There are picnic tables, lean-tos for camping, and drinking water at the hand pump.

Continue on the road that winds towards the look-out tower on Mount Rutsen. Watch on your left for a bedrock outcrop in the hillside. This was quarried, its stones used to build Suckley Chapel, which we'll talk about shortly.

Atop the tower are views through the trees of the Rhinecliff Bridge, the Hudson River, and the Catskills. The predecessor of this tower was built by the U.S. Army with Mr. Astor's permission, and manned during World War I to watch for enemy aircraft that might buzz up the river. On the south side of the tower is the stone foundation of John Jacob Astor's observation tower. Made of wood with a circular staircase up the center, it had been recently built when Astor torched a nearby farm. To accumulate his 2,800-acre estate, Astor had bought

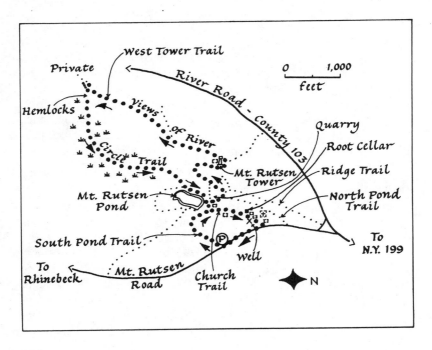

fifty-nine farms. One by one, he burned them. Staley's grandfather helped, but Astor preferred to do the torching himself. One fire got away from him, burned his new tower, and nearly all of Ferncliff Forest.

You can't see it from today's tower, but down the center of the Hudson River from Barrytown to Kingston for four and one half miles runs, underwater, a ridge called The Flats. In depths as shallow as two feet, The Flats contain mud bars and beds of wild celery and Eurasian water milfoil. It is one of the largest flats in the Hudson.

In mid-March the shad run from the Atlantic Ocean up the Hudson River. One of their primary destinations is The Flats. On The Flats' shoals and sandbars the silverbacks spawn, and during that time gill nets are forbidden on The Flats. The adults return by June to the Atlantic, leaving the young to hatch and mature into one of the largest commercial fisheries in the United States.

Other fish spawn here, among them striped bass and white perch. Shortnose and Atlantic sturgeon feed and rest in the adjacent deeper channels. From the tower on Mount Rutsen you might see large flocks of waterfowl that feed on the wild celery of The Flats: scaups, redhead, canvasback, common goldeneye, mergansers, mallard, black duck, and blue-winged teal.

Take the West Tower Trail. There are views through the trees of the Hudson River. The forest contains a well-developed shrub layer of mapleleaf viburnum (*Viburnum acerifolium*). To the uninitiated, this common local shrub is usually mistaken for scraggly young maple trees not worth a second glance. The leaf looks like a three-lobed red maple leaf. Feel one. It is velvety with hairs on the underside, not a maple at all. In June, the flat, white, viburnum flower heads bloom, ripening into blue-black berries in September that are eaten by ruffed grouse, deer, and red squirrel. In winter, the twigs are eaten by deer and rabbit. Autumn is my favorite time of year to see this shrub. Each leaf turns into a watercolor of rose, purple, lavender, white, bronze, peach, and even blue.

As of this writing, the trails are marked with bright yellow tops from Hershey's chocolate syrup cans. (A good idea, but someone's got one fantastic sweet tooth.) The West Tower Trail ends at three yellow tops. The road continues straight onto private property. Turn left onto the footpath through an old hemlock grove. This will bring you out to Mount Rutsen Pond.

Ferncliff Forest is an excellent birding area, especially for warblers.

Try your "spishing call" (see Bowdoin Park chapter) at the lake edge. Identifying these bright and perky mites, especially in fall when they sport their nonbreeding and juvenile plumage, has sent many an otherwise devoted bird watcher screaming from the woods, frothing at the mouth and swearing that they'll never again attempt to classify a warbler. My god, they all look alike! And there are so *many* of them!

Warblers breed and nest in America and Canada. Come fall, many of their brilliant yellows, reds, and oranges turn to a camouflage of olive-green, and they head south. During the daytime, they feed, still headed south tree by tree. Watch your backyard in migration time, and you'll see them darting and searching for food between the leaves of the canopy. A constant wave of warblers on the move lasts for weeks. At night, they fly at a great height, twittering. Their destination: Mexico, Guadeloupe, Venezuela, Ecuador, Nicaragua, Colombia, the Bahamas, the West Indies, and Panama. Our common, tiny, yellow warbler flies even to Brazil and Peru.

Circle the pond back to the maintenance shed. Take the Church Trail. How many foundations can you find? There are several old cellar holes, foundations, a well, and an old root cellar of local stone with a remarkable arched roof (they knew how to build them in those days).

Thomas Suckley of Wilderstein owned part of Ferncliff before John Jacob Astor. Methodist ministers in those days had very little pay and no retirement program. Suckley provided for them after their retirement. He allowed the elderly ministers to live on what is now Church Trail rent-free. He built several barns and a few two-story wood-frame houses, the root cellar, and the well. There was an icehouse by the pond. The ministers farmed the land and kept cows, pigs, and chickens. So that the ministers could continue to hold services, Suckley built a chapel in 1883, and often attended services there with his neighbors. Staley's father, uncle, and aunt went to church in Suckley Chapel. When wealthy Astor bought the property, the ministers had to leave. Astor drowned in the U.S.S. *Titanic* disaster.

Church Trail brings you out on Mount Rutsen Road. Turn right for a short walk to your car.

24. Ogden Mills and Ruth Livingston Mills State Historic Site and Park

Location: Staatsburg
Distance: 2 miles; 2 to 3 hours
Owner: State of New York

Mills Mansion and adjacent Norrie (see next walk) make one state park large enough for us to split them and take a walk in each. The extensive trail system of Mills-Norrie State Park explores deciduous woodlands, old estates, and the Hudson River shore.

There are two mansions at Mills State Historic Site: Mills Mansion and Hoyt House. Both contain grounds typical of their era: one says, "I am in control of the land"; the other says, "I am a part of the land."

Mills Mansion is New York's single largest state-owned historic building. In a word, it's immense. Sixty-five rooms, fourteen baths, in a seventy- by one-hundred-seventy-foot Beaux Arts extravaganza remodeled by the same folks who dreamed up Vanderbilt Mansion and the White House of Washington, D.C. The land was owned by the Livingston family beginning in 1844. The house and grounds, built in 1895, are an example of the gilded taste of the wealthiest class in America before the turn of the century.

Hoyt House, or The Point, is one of the most notable romantic era gardens in the nation. It was built around 1855 according to the principles of America's first landscape gardener, Andrew Jackson Downing, who also developed the first uniquely American style of architecture. From Newburgh, Downing laid out the original grounds (now gone) for the Capital, the White House, and the Smithsonian (he also designed the building). His "moonlight and roses" career was cut short when the steamship *Henry Clay* blew up on the Hudson

River. Downing was on board. Downing's partner, Calvert Vaux (who later persuaded Frederick Law Olmsted to join him in designing Manhattan's Central Park and Brooklyn's Prospect Park) designed The Point. Not just a "picturesque stone country house," as Vaux catalogued it but a complete landscape garden.

By garden, I do not mean peonies and pansies. According to Downing and Vaux, "garden" meant a serene and sublime total garden experience within which all American families would live happily in homes designed to be in harmony with their landscape; what they believed to be an architectural basis for a sane and solid national civilization.

Mills Mansion and Hoyt House are each the antithesis of the other. These two styles, the classical and the romantic, warred for decades. Both swept the Hudson Valley in the 1800s. The pendulum swung from the rustic Gothic Revival and Victorian styles to the opulent and lavish Greek Revival. In fact, the Livingstons parceled off The Point land from Mills Mansion land for their daughter, Geraldine, and her husband, Lydig Hoyt, both confirmed romantics.

In the end, the classical style won. Mills Mansion and its grounds stand preserved and honored. As a nation, we treasure the marble monuments and give little heed to the rustic. Hence Hoyt House has not yet been restored, and there are few of Downing's or Vaux's houses left intact.

ACCESS

Mills Mansion State Historic Site is located just north of the hamlet of Staatsburg. The entrance is off Old Post Road, but the grand way is from NY 9 through the golf course and the view of the Catskills. Cross the railroad tracks and park at the Mansion.

The grounds are open all year. Phone: office, (914) 889-4100 for information on when Mills Mansion is open.

TRAIL

There are two parking lots at Mills Mansion. Go to the one on the building's south side and stand at its southernmost edge looking south. Before you stretches a downslope of lawn, and in it grows an ancient black locust, slightly to your right. Pass to the right of this locust and continue straight to the tree line where a trail leads through a clove

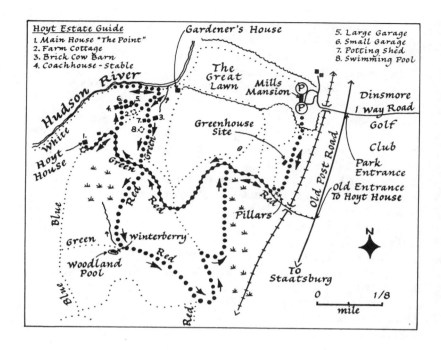

Hoyt Estate Guide

between two small knolls. Go past the hemlocks and the horse trail, keeping straight to a wide grassy area, once the site of the Mansion's greenhouse complex.

The trail turns right past two cement pillars, nonnative chestnuts, and osage orange trees. In about twenty feet the trail curves right again. On the left is a Norway maple with pachysandra beneath it. Go to the right of this maple, walk through the evergreen groundcover to the next Norway maple. See the cement cap on top of the stone wall slightly to your right? And the steppingstone shelf? This is an old footpath crossing. Go to it and over; there are two stepping shelves on the opposite side. Go through the woods to the road and turn right onto the red ski trail.

This is the entry road to Hoyt House, the finest feature of Calvert Vaux's romantic rural paradise. It winds and curves with the land-scape, undulating, creating an illusion of distance from hurried civilization. Keep straight on this drive. In its day, there were views that created natural and pastoral effects without any formal or grandly scaled manipulation of the landscape. The road curves sharply left uphill, and there is Hoyt House.

The circular, stone-lined driveway is practically invisible. The windows are boarded up. Succession is taking place on the lawns and the tremendous 180-degree view of the river is long grown up and gone. But still, what a place!

Sited on what may well be the finest piece of Hudson riverbank real estate sits an original Vaux landscape and house exterior *intact*. Hoyt House may look run-down, but the structure is solid, and eminently restorable. Imagine The Point as it was, the verandas cloaked in ornamental vines, the views from the rooms showing miles of river and hills. Look at the fine detail in the native dressed stones of the walls, subtly carved with stipples and striations to form a random and rustic pattern of texture.

To tour the rest of the estate, return down the entry drive and take your first left. The impressive west building was the coachhouse and stable. The other two were garages for automobiles, the larger of which houses an apartment overhead.

At the intersection, turn left, then right. Ahead is a three-story brick dairy barn that may date from 1855. Continue along the green trail, and you are in the midst of the farm complex, once lawn, today an overgrown tangle. Much labor and money is needed to keep an area halted at a particular successional stage. As soon as the input of energy ends, the inexorable march towards forest resumes.

In the center of the field is a long, narrow swimming pool, partially filled in and sprouting saplings. It was added to the estate in 1959. Rows of lilac and exotic cedar grow atop a brick-lined flower bed beside the greenhouse. Part of the wood frame of the greenhouse still stands, and beneath it is an exceptionally deep cellar. Not a trace remains of Vaux's wooden farm-tenant cottage.

Return to the blue trail and head for the Hudson River. The white trail that follows the river south to Norrie Point begins here under hemlocks. Walk down it a short distace to one of the points that stick out into the water. There are rocks on which to sit.

The Esopus Meadows Lighthouse out there in the middle of the river was one of the last manned lighthouses on the Hudson. Built in 1839 and rebuilt in 1872, it was one of nine Hudson River "family stations" under the jurisdiction of the U.S. Lighthouse Service. The various keepers and their families cleaned and tended the lens, living

In a boat you can get close enough to the Esopus Meadows Lighthouse to see that the "windows" are actually paintings on wood nailed over the real windows. Each "window" has a different painting.

for years in isolation out on the water in the white clapboard house built on a granite pier. Their logs report several large barges jammed against the house in storms. One winter, great ice sheets dislodged the structure from its foundation. Keeper John Kerr lived in the lighthouse with his wife, two pet skunks, a bantam rooster, and a dog. In 1939, the lighthouse came under the control of the U.S. Coast Guard. In 1965, Esopus Meadows Lighthouse was closed and automated.

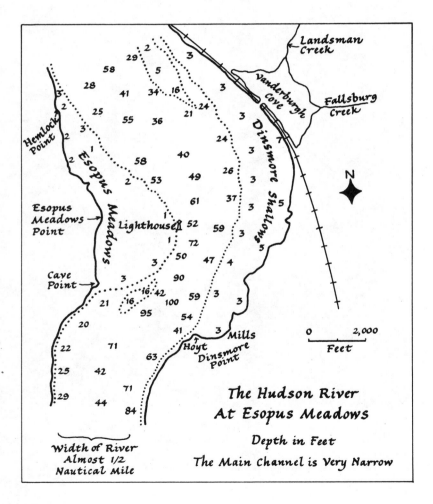

The Hudson River
At Esopus Meadows

Depth in Feet
The Main Channel is Very Narrow

Width of River
Almost 1/2
Nautical Mile

The lighthouse sits on the east edge of Esopus Meadows, a stretch of Hudson River three feet at its deepest. At low tide, you can see the grass, actually water celery, and Eurasian water milfoil. Just east of the lighthouse, the river bottom drops to fifty-two feet. Nearly all the Hudson River's shortnose sturgeon spend their winters in this narrow channel. Come spring, they swim north to Troy to spawn. Just east of where The Point juts out, the bottom rises again to the Dinsmore Shallows. This ecosystem, three to five feet deep, grows more grass, providing an important feeding and resting habitat for waterfowl and a spawning ground and nursery for large numbers of anadromous fishes.

Esopus, originally pronounced either *SHO-pus* or *SO-pus,* may be an archaic Munsee form for "creek." Such words include *ship-O-shesh* ("little creek"), *sip-O-sis, SOP-siw,* and *w-SO-psiw.* The last means, "person from *SO-pus,*" though some Lenape translate this as "person who is naked." *SEE-pu* is the contemporary word for "creek" or "river," so an Esopus Indian would have simply meant a lowlander or river Indian.

The blue trail leads to the Gardener's House. From here, you can stroll up the lawn to Mills Mansion.

Or, take the green trail to the red, into the woods. At the intersection, stay on the red, past the woodland pool where winterberry (*Ilex verticillata*) blooms. All winter, the branches hold their brilliant red berries without which, in summer, one might mistake this American holly for speckled alder.

Watch carefully for the left turn onto a horse trail, and a right after that, which will lead you past a loosestrife swamp to the Hoyt entry drive.

25. Margaret Lewis Norrie State Park

Location: Staatsburg
Distance: 3 miles; 3 to 4 hours
Owner: State of New York

If you've already walked Norrie's resplendent and wild white trail along the Hudson's bank (be certain to do so with He Who Stands Firm's guided trail leaflet in hand, available from the park), then try this walk to the lost mansions.

ACCESS

The park entrance is off U.S. 9 just south of Staatsburg. For our Lost Mansions walk, follow the signs for the picnic area and park in its lot. Phone: park office, (914) 889-4646.

TRAIL

A dirt road begins at the north end of the parking lot. Head downhill through oaks and black birch toward the sound of boats on the river. At the swing set, turn left, and go beneath the swings straight for the river. Choose the path that leads downhill and left under witch hazel bushes along an old broken metal fence until you hit the cove. Slide on down the eroded cleft to the pebble beach. Centuries of wave action have rounded the pebbles. The impressive building on the west shore is Mount St. Alphonsus Seminary, and the hill behind it is Shaupeneak. Around the cove and all along the Hudson's bank, hemlocks and northern white cedar darken the shoreline, their gnarled roots twisted in the rocks.

Northern white cedar (*Thuja occidentalis*) attracted legion European sailors and financiers to North America. Straight, tall, strong, northern white cedar could be cut into unparalleled masts, especially valued by admirals for their navies. The scales of the leaves are flattened, unlike the rounder, stiffer red cedar of sunny fields. Other than on the

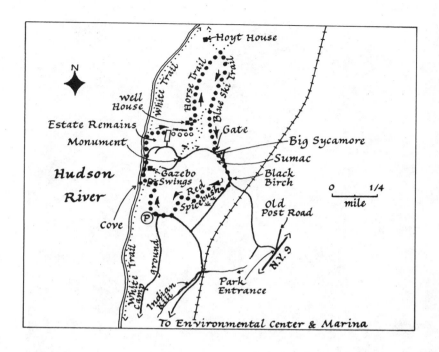

Hudson River shore, there is only one place in the Hudson Valley where one finds northern white cedar: the planted rows of old grave-yards.

Mahicanituk is one of the Hudson's original names, which in all dialects means, "Tidal River of the Mahican People." Watch the water. Which way is the tide going? Can you spot where the main channel flows? Why is the water so dirty?

Polluted is the better word for the sewage, pesticides, and vastly assorted chemicals in the waters and bottom silt. But the dirt? The Hudson has probably always looked a dirty green-brown. Twice a day the tides stir up sediments that never get a chance to settle. Turbid, ecologists call such murky water. Perfectly natural. A soup of organic and inorganic debris that is the basis for the food chain of the rich Hudson River Estuary. Swedish naturalist Peter Kalm reported in 1749 that the residents of Albany drew their drinking water directly from the Hudson, but the water was so muddy they had to store it in their cellars so the sediment could settle to the bottom.

Return to the trail and head upriver, or really, we should say, up-

Summer sunlight through witch hazel leaves.

estuary. The white trail soon leads to a paved road. Go past the gazebo. As the road leaves the river's edge, watch for a four-foot high granite pillar. This is the white trail again. Just past the pillar the trail forks. Take the left.

The deepest stone foundations were commercial ice houses, tall things that housed blocks of ice cut from the Hudson. "On both sides of the river one sees great numbers of monolithic icehouses which border, during the wintertime, those fields of ice that furnish such an abundant harvest," wrote Emile de Damseaux, a French traveler in 1877. The blocks were kept insulated with a covering of sawdust. Pass retaining walls and terraces; the remains of rich living. Iris, peony, rose, daylily, vinca, and other horticultural species survive in the lost garden. Go up stone stairs past forsythia. The white trail continues on along the water. We turn right up the stone path past honeysuckle and lily of the valley to the dirt parking lot.

Now you have a choice. You can either follow the paved road or bushwhack to our destination. The road is actually the harder of the two because of the maze of paths you must take. Better to bushwhack.

From the trail at the parking lot, keep straight across the lot (away from the river) and follow the stone wall. Easy to do. When it peters out, you'll be at an old dump. See the chipped blue and white plates, the rusted metal, the thick green glass bottles? Before you rises a steep slope. Climb up it. On top turn left.

Do you see it? The European castle-style well house, all stone, brick-trimmed windows, and slates on the roof. Alone atop a resistant bedrock hillock in the middle of the forest, abandoned and immense. One big room, its innards said to be lined in tile. Pipes lead off in all directions. From this one well house, water was supplied to a number of estate houses on the Hudson's bank. Walk *completely* around the house to a cliff-drop edge and take a rough path that leads along the edge and away from the house. When you step upon a piece of bedrock and a forked oak trunk is on your left, the path turns right and loops around to join a marked horse trail.

If you don't care to bushwhack and do not mind a longer way, then from the parking lot follow the paved road past the granite pillars that were once connected by chains. At the monument to young Lewis Gordon Norrie's happy youth, turn left onto the hemlock-lined dirt road. At the fork go left and step over the log. The well house will appear among the trees on your left. Go on up to it and explore.

At the base of the well house (as you face away from it), turn left onto the horse trail. At the intersection, you can turn left for a visit to Hoyt House and the labyrinth of Mills Mansion's trails. Or, turn right onto a dirt road and pass a young woods of closely packed saplings. On the right, watch through the stems for one huge oak, perhaps as much as 200 years old.

At the intersection with the green ski trail, bushwhack right and you'll come upon tennis courts, moss green on the edges. Back on the trail, keep straight. Pass honeysuckle, non-native conifers, and exotics from another lost estate. You are now on the blue ski trail.

At the gate, turn left onto the paved road. Keep right, past autumn's red berries of staghorn and smooth sumac (*Rhus typhina* and *glabra*). Float these berries in warm water to brew lemonade. Find the bluebird nesting box on the right. Black birch (*Betula lenta*) grows beside and beyond it; the tree with the shiny black bark and the horizontal lenticel lines. Break off a twig and smell. Menthol? Chew. Wintergreen!

Turn right at the next paved road to return to the picnic area. Twenty feet from the intersection, find the red trail in the trees on your right. Follow through woods, over wood planks on the edge of a swamp, up a hill, and over stone walls. At the top of the hill, when you've got a stone wall to your left, spicebush (*Lindera benzoin*) grows on both sides of the trail. It's the bush with the brown twigs, green at the tips, and the raised dots on the bark. Break off a twig. Smell. Lemons? Chew. Oooof! Strong stuff. What can I say, some folks like it. European colonists dried and pulverized the bark and berries for a spice. Both spicebush and black birch twigs can be steeped in boiling water to make teas. The flavors come from chemicals manufactured by the plants and stored in the inner bark and cambium layers, beneath the outer bark and before the wood.

The trail wends uphill past woodland pools, swamps, and woods. At the paved road turn right, and there's your car. You can extend your walk by continuing on the red trail to Dutchess Community College's Environmental Center, where there are exhibits and aquariums. Return along the paved road or the white trail.

26. Vanderbilt Mansion National Historic Site

Location: Hyde Park
Distance: 2.5 miles; 2 hours
Owner: National Park Service

Through the stone arches of the main gate, over the formal White Bridge topped with urns and flowers, past the waterfall, and up the long grassy lawn, the Mansion looms ahead. Built of grey-white Indiana limestone at a cost of $660,000, the 1898 palace of Frederick W. Vanderbilt sits in the center of a 212-acre sculpted and wild estate.

ACCESS

Vanderbilt Mansion is just north of the village of Hyde Park on U.S. 9. Phone: the visitors' center, (914) 229-9115.

TRAIL

Park in the visitors' center lot. The trees around this building are described in a guide, "Trees of the Vanderbilt Estate," available from the visitors' center desk. The planting of exotics was begun on the grounds in 1828 by the previous owner, Dr. David Hosack, whose landscaping won the property international renown. It's worth a trip to Vanderbilt's just to explore the lawns and the many strange and ancient trees. Our walk begins along the paved North Drive beneath sugar maples, basswood, oak, white pine, and imported firs. Head left (north) of the visitors' center, being careful of occasional traffic.

Crickets sing in the grasses as you walk the east bluff of the Hudson River. The view is a famous one: grass slopes away to woods, the blue Hudson River, and hills and the Catskills on the opposite shore—obscured in a summer haze or sharply defined when there is a wind. Head toward Bard Rock. Before the road curves downhill toward the river, there will be a plantation of white pine on your left. Walk in under the first trees and find the path that follows along the bluff edge.

Curve down the slope with the pines and rejoin the paved road. Follow past the meadows and locust trees to a dirt road on the left hung with the sign: "Service Road Only." Put on the mosquito repellent and take the dirt road into the woods.

Where the Norway spruce stand ends, the straightest, tallest, highest trees on the left are tulip (*Liriodendron tulipifera*), a tree prized for ship masts and dugout canoes. Tulip tree leaves are distinctive. On younger saplings they're often as large as plates.

In June, tulip trees bear flowers that look exactly like green and yellow tulips with orange centers, but they bloom high up, visible from the ground only as bright vases. Should you find one fallen, you'll see the many long male stamens that bear the pollen. In their center sits the fat female pistil. Pollen from the male stamens falls onto the female pistil and fertilizes her eggs. Functions completed,

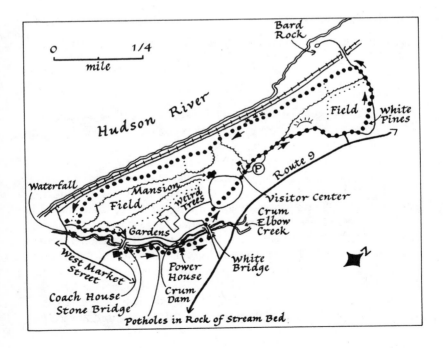

the petals and the stamens fade and fall to the ground. The eggs mature into seeds.

In autumn, you'll see the candelabra seed heads high up where the flowers bloomed. On a windy, winter day, the seeds blow down and can be found on the snow. Native Americans cooked the fat sticky green buds of spring into a salve for burns and scalds. The inner bark of tulip is white, and so strong it can be twisted into cordage.

Just before the lawn, a small trail breaks through the iron rail fence that separates the estate from the railroad. Go through it and you have a cliff-top view of the river, the railroad, Bard Rock, and the opposite hills. Lowbush blueberries grow here. Visit in July and enjoy! Bracken fern and sassafras indicate a well-drained soil. Bracken fern can be gathered dry in autumn, stuffed into cloths to make mattresses. Sassafras bears three leaf shapes on one plant: round, mitten, and three-lobed hand.

The majestic mansion sits up on the hill. Half the fun of this walk is seeing the columned house from different angles and settings.

Beyond the planted vinca, watch on the left for bladdernut bushes. The inflated seed pods hang like balloons, green in June, brown and rattling by August. Beyond the bladdernuts comes another break in the iron-rail fence with another view from a cliff top.

As you come out to the paved road, you'll hear the waterfall ahead. Crum Elbow Creek splashes noisy and wide over a concrete lip onto boulders and cliff. The name comes from *kromme hoek*, rounded corner, which later became *krom elleboge*, or crooked elbow, a name given by Dutch settlers to a point and a bend in the Hudson River, just south of where this stream has its mouth. Walk across the lawn to see the falls, then follow the road uphill. There are long vistas down the "English country park" fields.

In the pond above the falls look for snapping turtles. Snappers get big. In the water they look like logs or rocks up to a foot and a half across. Two nostrils at the tip of the nose and an enormously long neck allow a snapper to peek up for a breath of air without exposing its tremendous body—no teeth, but a sharp beak and strong jaws, and powerful legs with stout claws. In the open water of ponds and lakes of any size, they float. As youngsters they eat meat; as adults they incorporate plants into fully one-half of their diet. Occasionally, they seize a duckling by the feet to drown and devour. Should you be swimming and accidentally step on one in the murk of the shallows, it'll pull in its head, shut its eyes, and wait for you to step off. In a pond, its maneuverability, the murky water, and the pond bottom provide a snapper with all the safety it needs, and it's a pussycat.

On land it's another story. Snappers hiss. They lunge. And they snap. That long neck reaches halfway back along the shell for a bite. A snapper on land is vulnerable. Unlike most turtles, the snapper has only a tiny plastron, or bottom shell. It may try to pull in its legs, head, and tail, but nothing happens. There's nowhere to go. The meaty legs, abdomen, chest, neck, and head are all exposed. Vulnerability is why a snapper snaps on land. For greater mobility on land, it gave up its protective large bottom shell and developed in its place a protective behavior.

Stroll up the road lined with sugar maples. Above the pond, Crum Elbow Creek runs through a hemlock gorge of mossy and fractured bedrock. Walk out to the middle of the stone bridge for a view of the deep pools and rapids in both directions. If you are pooped, return to the road and head toward the mansion and your car. If, on the other hand, you're ready for adventure, the best is saved for last. Cross the bridge and turn left on the path.

Look back at the bridge. It's enchanting. Two arches of round glacial cobbles and rough-broken stone. Follow the path upstream through the cool, splashing gorge. The stream evens out to quiet pools and rills, a good place to watch for mated pairs of ducks and their ducklings. The trail becomes a sort of stone wall bank.

Crum Dam's waterfall frames the pond beyond, and beyond that is the stately White Bridge and its waterfall. Atop the bank is the stone powerhouse. Our trail narrows and becomes a steep edge. Just continue on along the water past the powerhouse. Should you be too nervous for this route, scramble up the wall to the powerhouse itself and walk along the bank top. The trail there leads to the same place in a few safer yards.

Watch the pond for ducks and bluegill. Just before the White Bridge, beeches stand carved with initials, the sad fate of smooth-skinned beeches that grow where people frequent. Turn left onto the bridge. Halfway across look down at the water. In summer, flocks of blue damselflies will be winging on the hunt. Cross the bridge, turn right at the catalpa and follow the gravel path to the mansion lawn. Cut across the lawn to reach your car.

The other way is to follow the road up the hill from the bridge, turn left, and visit the formal perennial and rose gardens. Spectacular in summer. To end your adventure, stroll the lawns, marvel at the

View from the mansion down the English park lawn to the Hudson River.

strange trees with limbs so old and low they lie on the ground and sprout trunks: hemlock, Norway spruce, and white fir. Enjoy the gigantic weeping beech (be sure to duck beneath its limbs and go inside to see its snaking trunks) and the odd ginkgo. Rest behind the mansion upon a bench and admire the view. Go ahead, stand on the portico with the wind and dream of industrial and financial empire.

At the northwest corner of the mansion on the bank edge grows a tulip tree with branches so low that in June you get a chance to see, smell, and feel, within reach, a tulip-tree tulip.

27. Franklin D. Roosevelt National Historic Site

Location: Hyde Park
Distance: 2.75 miles; 3 hours
Owner: National Park Service

There are the tame fields, the gardens, the lawns, Springwood (the mansion), the presidential library, and the various estate buildings. That's what most visitors see. Then there are the old growth hemlock stands and the acres of wild ravines near the Hudson River. One hundred eighty-eight acres total.

ACCESS

Franklin D. Roosevelt National Historic site is located on U.S. 9 in Hyde Park. From the entrance, drive straight back toward the handicapped parking area past rows of ornamental cherry trees. Park at the extreme southwestern corner of the lot. The grounds are open from 9 AM to dusk. Phone: park offices (914) 229-9115.

TRAIL

Look for two signs: a green "Authorized Vehicles Only" and a brown "Private Residence" at the head of a paved road. Take this road. It curves first left, away from the private residence (a grey wood structure with delicate millwork), then forks. At the fork is a map for the Hudson River Trail. Take the right fork downhill under hemlocks.

At the next fork, stop and, if it is summer, arm yourself with mosquito repellent. Take the dirt road that forks left.

An alternate and more exciting beginning is to leave your car in the same place, walk up to the library, stroll by the gravesite to the house and right past onto the lawn. What a view. There's the trough where the Hudson flows, the hills of Ulster, and the apple orchard at your

144

feet. Enjoy the breeze for one last time, protect yourself with repellent, and plunge down the steep grassy slope into the orchard. Cut straight through.

Either way you'll end up on the dirt River Road. If you're coming directly down the road from the parking lot, listen for the sound of not the first but the second brook that runs through the grasses and bubbles under the road through a culvert. Mint grows on the left side where the brook disappears underground. If they've been mowing, you'll smell it. Feel a stem. Members of the mint family have square stems. This is the sort of mint to float a few leaves of in a pitcher of pink lemonade. Take the right fork into the woods. If you've come from the house, be sure to find this turn-off.

In summer, the female deerflies will greet you. Great trail buddies, they follow and circle your head for as long as you walk the woods. While their males are off frequenting flowers, the females patrol for blood. Bodies gold and black, wings striped with brown, they hover

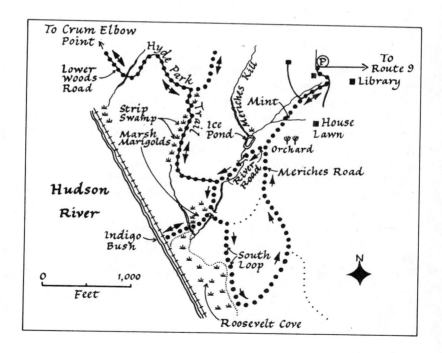

over the trails where they know from past experience a full-blooded creature will come sooner or later. Their bite is painful, and their buzzing and swooping annoying. A hat is about the best you can do; that'll keep them off your scalp. Unfortunately, it won't get rid of them. A small consolation is knowing that it's much worse for the deer than for you.

The hemlocks are cool and dark. In a short while a side trail forks off to your right and leads to the ice pond. Throughout the Hudson Valley, ice cutting was big business, most of the ice being packed and shipped to New York City. Some even went as far as the West Indies. The wealthy could afford their own ice ponds, which also made for good swimming in summer.

Back on the road, the trail follows the stream. Northern copperheads live in these woods, preferring the sunny rock outcrops at the top of the hills. Unless you go bushwhacking, you're not likely to encounter one. But should you see a snake, copperheads are unmistakable. Pictures and photographs rarely do them justice. Their heads are bright red-copper, like an Irish lass's hair. Their bodies have bright copper, dog-bone patterns against a lighter brown background. Despite this metallic coloration, copperheads are so well camouflaged against brown leaves that they usually go unnoticed.

The head is triangular, the poison glands being located at the base of the triangle. Nonpoisonous snakes who lack such glands have round heads. Get close enough to a copperhead (that is caged or dead) and you'll see the dark vertical slit for a pupil and, between the nostril and the eye, another hole. This is the pit. The copperhead is a pit viper. With this sensory organ, the snake in the black of night can see its prey by the infrared heat of the prey's body.

Copperhead poison is a blood toxin. A mouse bitten by a copperhead runs. The poison is pumped throughout its body, and shortly, the mouse drops dead. The copperhead follows the mouse's heat trail, locates it by smell (using its forked tongue which withdraws into the mouth into two holes called Jacobson's organ), and swallows it whole, head first.

A human infant bitten by a copperhead is in mortal danger. An adult bitten by a copperhead is in more danger of nausea from a hospital's antivenin shot. Each year many nonvenomous snakes, thought to be copperheads, are killed. Unfortunate, seeing as how copperheads are mostly gentle, lethargic serpents content to lie motionless and hunt mice.

146

At the fork, turn right onto Lower Woods Road. This is the Hyde Park Trail that links the Roosevelt site with Vanderbilt mansion. If you proceed on it a short way, turning left at a fork, left at another fork, and then crossing the trail trestle, you will come to Crum Elbow Point, a rocky bluff with a river view. Unfortunately, the Hyde Park Trail makes no loop since the connections run onto private property. You'll have to retrace your steps to River Road. Both forks of Lower Woods Road are worth the trip. Of special interest is the strip swamp covered with duck weed. In spring come see the breeding spotted newts. Red ash *(Fraxinus pennsylvanica)* is the slim, straight tree that grows in the water with the swollen trunk base and a compound leaf of seven leaflets.

The trail winds through hemlocks, steep ravines, outcrops of bedrock, brooks, and hollows. At the bottom of every hollow lies a black pool of water. Some keep their water all year. Others are filled only

The view downriver at Crum Elbow in the Hudson River.

in spring. These vernal woodland pools are the breeding centers for wood frog, toads, spring peeper, spotted and Jefferson salamanders, and fairy shrimp. Come June, the amphibian larvae have either matured and fled or died, and the fairy shrimp larvae have matured and burrowed for the remainder of the year into the pool mud. Slowly, the pool dries, until all that is left is a black mat of dried dead leaves.

Next spring, rains refill the pool. The first steamy, warm rainy night of spring brings a mass movement of amphibians back to the pools of their birth. So also did their parents return to the same pool, and their parents before them, on down the ancestral line. Returning all on one night, in the mist and the rain, to lie in writhing mats of mass mating orgies.

Back on River Road, walk out of the hemlocks into sunlight and a swamp. Come in May to see the marsh marigolds (*Caltha palustris*). No flower—neither buttercup nor England's celandine—blooms a petal so glossy gold-yellow as marsh marigold.

The stream empties into Roosevelt Cove, an inlet of the Hudson subject to the Hudson's tides. Cattail, arrowhead, wild rice, and spatterdock clog the inlet in warm weather. At the trail end sign and gate, head straight over the railroad tracks for the Hudson. (Be careful! Amtrak comes through here quietly at more than seventy miles per hour.)

Downriver are the Railroad and Mid-Hudson Bridges. And yes, the deerflies are gone! This is a good spot to come in winter to see the ice floes.

As you face the river, on your right, past the silky dogwood, grows dull-leaf indigo bush (*Amorpha fruticosa*). Tropical-looking. In June, indigo-purple spikes bloom fringed with yellow anthers. To your left grows ninebark (*Physocarpus opulifolius*). Clustered white flowers in early June mature into green and salmon-pink dry bladders. The older twigs are rough with wings of cork.

Take the South Loop for the return. The deerflies will accompany you until you hit pavement.

28. Locust Grove

Location: Poughkeepsie
Distance: 3.5 miles; 2 hours
Owner: Young-Morse Historic Site

Telegraph inventor and portrait painter Samuel F. B. Morse bought Locust Grove, a Livingston property for many years, in 1847 as a summer home. In 1901, the estate was sold to the wealthy Poughkeepsie family of William Hopkins Young and Martha Innis Young. The site is now a registered National Historic Landmark open to the public.

The grounds contain 150 acres of woodland historically farmed, pastured, and landscaped for carriage rides. It is a pretty place to walk in spring or autumn. Be sure to bring mosquito repellent if you visit in summer.

ACCESS

Locust Grove is located 2 miles south of the Mid-Hudson Bridge on U.S. 9. The entrance is on the west side of U.S. 9 at a stoplight just north of the Hudson and Poughkeepsie Mall plazas, and just south of Poughkeepsie Rural Cemetery. The house and grounds are open Memorial Day through September, Wednesday through Sunday, 10 AM to 4 PM, all holidays during the open season, and weekends in October. Admission fees to the house are adults $4, seniors $3.50, and children $1. Admission to the grounds is free. Phone: office (914) 454-4500.

TRAIL

Most visitors see only the house of Locust Grove. The estate trails and old carriage roads are little used and, in summer, can get overgrown. Wear long pants when you come. From the parking lot, walk past the cottage through the gardens to the Tuscan Villa–style house. The trail begins on the north side of the house as a dirt road that

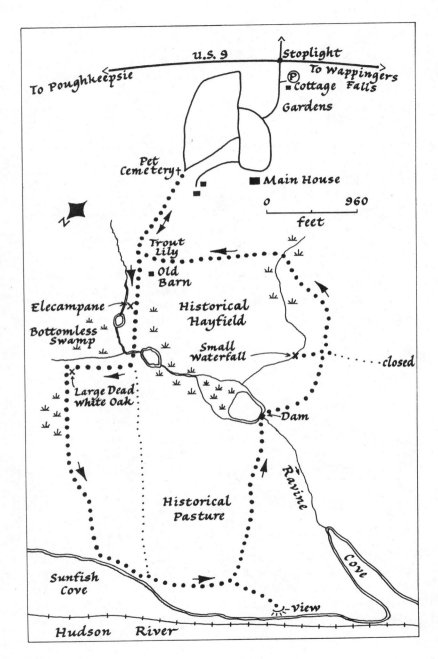

passes a pet cemetery and leads downhill through a typical mixed deciduous forest of large tulip, Norway and sugar maple, black birch, hickory, locust, beech, ash, and witch hazel. If you walk here in early May, you will find that—as with Reese Sanctuary in Wappingers Falls—summer has already arrived. The Norway maples are leafed out, the veery sings silver waterfalls, and the air brushes your cheek as a perfumed breeze.

At the fork, bear right past the old barn and hayrake. The stone wall that borders the trail is built in the flat-top style of an estate boundary marker, quite unlike the jumbled stone walls of a farmer's fields. Off in the woods on your right, the thick and tall yellow daisy from England, elecampane, blooms in early August. One of the most famous of ancient medicines, the root, according to Hippocratic writings, is a powerful stimulant to the brain, stomach, kidneys, and uterus.

At the next intersection, turn right past the Bottomless Swamp. One winter's day somewhere between 1900 and 1910, some people out for a drive thought they might take their carriage straight across this swamp. The carriage sunk in and never was recovered, giving the swamp its name.

Some hemlock occurs in these woods, along with many horticultural escapees: Japanese barberry, Japanese knotweed, Norway maple, vinca, and pachysandra. When the numerous native, flowering dogwoods and witch hazels bloom, they make the subcanopy layer stand out distinctly. Spicebush and skunk cabbage mark the wetlands.

The trail leads out to a view through the trees of the Hudson River and Sunfish Cove. Follow along the river bluff under red oak and white pine. At the fork, turn right. The trail narrows. Follow it all the way to the pitch pine at the top of the cliff whose carbonate face in May is covered with columbine. Downriver is the Pirate Canoe Yacht Club, upriver the Mid-Hudson and Cantilever Bridges. One cannot see farther north or south, because this stretch of river runs straight for so great a distance that Robert Juet, a mate on board Henry Hudson's *Half Moon*, named this long, straight stretch Lange Rack, or Long Reach. It runs from about Danskammer Point to the lower end of Crum Elbow. A sailing ship could navigate this impressively long straight sailing course with only one setting of the boom. North of the bridges, you can see the river turning to the left; that is the stretch called Crum Elbow.

The best and easiest view to be had of the entire Long Reach is

Hudson River fisherman with a young Hudson River sturgeon.

from the Mid-Hudson Bridge. As you drive across, you can see straight downriver, down the Long Reach, to Danskammer Point and, if it is a clear day, the Beacon Range on the horizon. Upriver, the Hudson curves west into Crum Elbow.

From Vanderbilt Mansion to Bowdoin Park, through Crum Elbow and the Lange Rack, runs the Poughkeepsie Deepwater Habitat, a fourteen-mile, nearly continuous river-bottom trench 30 to 125 feet deep. Such deepwater estuaries are rare in the eastern United States. The endangered shortnose sturgeon spawns and winters here, along with large numbers of anchovy, silverside, bluefish, weakfish, and hogchoker.

Return to the trail and turn right to continue beneath a canopy of witch hazel and then along the top of a deciduous ravine. In summer in these moist woods you may hear a trilling up in the trees, always a few trees or more away, never very close. These are grey treefrogs, amphibians found throughout the eastern woodlands. At the ends of their long flexible fingers are tree-climbing pads. Most likely, you'll never see one; though large as wood frogs, their skin is patterned like gray and green army camouflage. As soon as you come close to zeroing in on their tree, they clam up. Even should you locate the tree they're in, they blend in so perfectly you might be looking right at one and not notice.

At the head of the ravine, cross the stone dam. At the four-way intersection, take the left path past purple and yellow early woodland violets to a little waterfall that curtains over an outcrop of bedrock, then return and turn left on the dirt road. As the trail curves toward the house (you'll see the Tuscan tower), the bank on your right in mid- to late April will be covered in trout lily, but by mid-May, it will be dying and soon gone. *Erythronium americanum* is also known as dog-toothed violet, or adder's tongue. The leaves are shiny, leathery, green mottled with purple-brown, one leaf per bulb. When the lily bulb reaches maturity in seven or more years, it grows two leaves and blooms. The flowers are yellow, down-draped bells fringed on the inside with orange and purple-pollened stamens. They last perhaps a week, then wither.

The spring rains of April trickling through the soil could leach out the nutrients essential for healthy forest growth. *Erythronium* and a few other spring woodland flowers, such as hepatica and anemone, are the only plants active at this time. Growing in carpets that blanket the forest floor, *Erythronium* roots absorb quantities of the soil nutrients before they can be leached away and store them in their purple and green leaves. The leaves photosynthesize until the tree buds break out overhead in the tree canopy. Once the full sunlight gets shut out, *Erythronium* withers and dies. As it decays, the stored nutrients are released, just in time for the burst of tree activity and growth that needs them. The *Erythronium* bulbs expand underground, then go dormant in the soil until next April.

The road curves to rejoin the entrance trail and you are back at the house.

29. Bowdoin Park

Location: Wappingers Falls
Distance: 2 miles; 2 hours
Owner: County of Dutchess

This riverside county park contains 301 acres of woods, ball fields, sledding hills, and picnic facilities, along with a fine nature and cultural museum. The woods contain typical Hudson River shore bottomland and upland species, and a Native American rock shelter.

ACCESS

From U.S. 9, there are several ways to get onto Sheafe Road. One way is from the north end of the Galleria Mall. Turn west onto Spring Road. At the stop sign turn left onto Sheafe Road. Bowdoin is 2.3 miles down Sheafe Road, on the right. Park at the museum/administration building lot by the flag pole and the public phone. Phone: park office, (914) 297-1224.

TRAIL

From the parking lot, you can see the "castle," a looming structure of smokestacks and squares on the west bank of the Hudson River. When the sun's behind it, it looks black. This is Central Hudson Gas & Electric Corporation's Danskammer coal/oil plant that, along with the Roseton plants, supply electricity to many counties.

In 1663, Lieutenant Cowenhoven, a Dutch skipper, saw Indians dancing by firelight on a flat rock, acres wide, that jutted into the Mahicanituk, the "tidal river of the Mahican" Native People. He named the place *duyvel's danskammer*, or "devil's dancehall." The Native People had, of course, no concept concerning any devil, let alone devil dances.

Danskammer was a unique rock. Henry Hudson and Peter Kalm saw it; Washington Irving wrote about it. Benson Lossing described it in 1866 as a rock with "a level surface of about half an acre (now

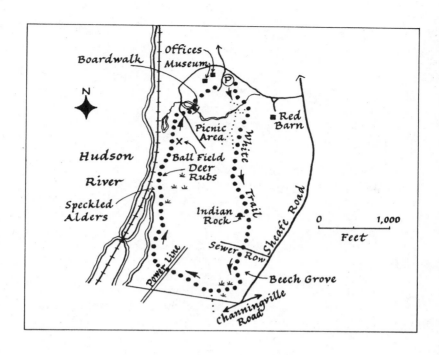

covered with beautiful Arbor Vitae shrubs), and is separated from the main-land by a marsh. On this rock the Indians performed their peculiar semi-religious rites, called *pow-wows*, before going upon hunting and fishing expeditions, or the war-path."

The Native People used the rock for at least a century after the coming of Europeans. What was seen at this rock—said to have been perfectly level and only two or three feet above the Hudson waterline—was probably one of the annual thanksgiving ceremonies honoring the Creator and lesser spirits, perhaps the annual Green Corn Dance. The nineteenth-century historian Edward Ruttenber writes in his *History of the Indian Tribes of Hudson's River* that up to 500 Munsee and Esopus peoples could be there at one time, "kinte-kaying," dancing. *Kuhntke* is Lenape for "dancing and singing at the same time" with overall spiritual connotations. The area also seems to have been a general congregating spot for European social parties as well as for Natives on fishing trips. Wallace Bruce in 1907 described the Danskammer as easily visible from the Hudson River Day Line steamers: "a large flat rock, covered with cedars, recently marked by a lighthouse."

On top this unique jut of bedrock was built the Danskammer power plant. Robert Boyle, who calls such things "hellish plants," would likely say Danskammer is finally appropriately named.

Our walk begins opposite the parking lot on top of a grassy bank. A sign and a map stand at the head of the Edna C. MacMahon Nature Trail.

As you walk the trail, you'll see myrtle, horse chestnut, Japanese honeysuckle, yew, and other horticultural leftovers from the Hudson River estate that became Bowdoin Park. In April, Dutchman's breeches, red trillium, hepatica, and trout lily bloom under the oaks and sugar maples.

At Indian Rock, walk out to the edge of the cliff for an open view of the river. From this point, there are few signs of humans: nearly no houses and no industry. Even the busy traffic sounds of the river are buffered and seem gone. In winter, there is usually an interspecies flock feeding in the trees. Black-capped chickadees, nuthatches, titmice, and downy woodpeckers band together for the duration of the winter months, communally searching for food and keeping an eye out for predators. Listen for their "chick-a-dee-dee-deee" and nasal nuthatch "naa-naa" calls. These birds respond well to the "spishing call." Stand stock-still and say: "spish, spish, spish," just with the lips, as though you were calling a kitty. If you must move, do so in slow motion. "Spish, spish, spish," and chickadees often dive right out of the trees to take a look at you.

In this quiet, remote-seeming spot, it is easy to imagine Indian Rock as the Native American shelter it is. Each time some new industry breaks ground on the banks of the Mahicanituk, the Hudson, scores of Native artifacts and the debris of entire habitations are found. All sites along the Hudson River were heavily used from prehistoric to colonial times by the Native People. It was a hunter's and gatherer's paradise. The Hudson River was (and still is) a highway and a supermarket filled with—to name a few delicacies—striped bass, shad, sturgeon, alewives, oysters, clams, duck potato, water lily, bulrushes, and cattails.

Indian Rock and another Bowdoin site beside the river were excavated, and it is not surprising to find, through the study of the numerous knives, scrapers, projectile points, hammers, pottery shards, and bone fragments found there, that the park was in continuous use from as early as 3500 B.C. Hunters and gatherers lived beneath the overhang of the North Bowdoin Rock Shelter on and off for 5,000 years.

To get down to the shelter, backtrack and take the side trail on your left. If this trail is hard to find, simply follow around the base of the cliff downhill to the overhanging shelter. Doesn't look like much of a home? Well, part of the overhang has fallen over the centuries. Yet, if you lived all your life outdoors, you'd say this was a snug place indeed, with perfect access to both the river and the happy hunting grounds of the hills. The rock is white and grey Pine Plains dolostone, a gritty, sedimentary, dolomitic limestone, in which part of the limestone or calcium carbonate has been replaced by magnesium carbonate.

Back on the white trail, continue across a stone wall, down a knoll, and bear right. At the grassy sewer-line right-of-way, continue directly across for the white trail. You'll come to a beech grove with a shrub layer of spicebush.

Go down a steep hill to a black willow swamp. In summer at this

View from behind the nature museum across the Hudson to "The Castle" at Danskammer Point.

spot, try out your "spishing call." Sparrows and bright tropically colored warblers will wing at you and perch in the bushes flicking their tails and furiously sounding alarm clicks. At the trail junction, turn right toward the river, keeping on the white trail. This takes you under the power line, a place overgrown with multiflora rose, blackberry, and maples and oaks suckering up from cut stumps. Listen for sparrows, juncos (in winter), and cardinals. As you approach the inlet, keep a sharp eye out for waterfowl; they may spook before you get to see them. Kingfishers, mallards, herons, and geese are almost always somewhere on the water. If you venture out onto the mud, you may find deer tracks and the four-pronged, black seed cases (caltrops) of water chestnut, an introduced waterway pest.

Just beyond the foot bridge on the left are some large speckled alder bushes. The long male catkins release yellow pollen in spring, which fertilizes the female cones. On the right grow bladderbushes.

With a brackish marsh on the left and a freshwater marsh on the right, what better place to look for deer signs? Over half the bush stems for yards on the right are scarred with old and new deer-rub marks, from bucks scuffing the velvet off their antlers.

The trail leads out to the playing fields. As you walk back, you have a view of the river and the cliffs on the left and a view of the ridge you just walked on the right. Notice the differences in tree canopy silhouettes.

On the way back, be sure to walk across the boardwalk at the pond. This place takes much abuse, but the purple loosestrife (another introduced species) blooms prettily, and the water supports a population of painted turtles, snapping turtles, pet carp that people have released into the pond, and bluegill. Walk up the long grassy hill. Beneath the imported Douglas fir trees is your best view of the Danskammer "castle."

Be sure to stop in and visit the nature museum and the cultural museum. There are fine exhibits on Hudson River Valley ecology, anthropology, and archaeology, along with many live wild animals and some of the artifacts excavated at Indian Rock. On the way out you'll pass the Red Barn, which is maintained by the Boy Scout Explorers and houses barnyard and domestic animals.

30. Reese Sanctuary

Location: Wappingers Falls
Distance: 1.5 miles; 2 hours
Owner: National Audubon Society

Reese Sanctuary is a ninety-eight-acre woodland corridor on top the west bluff of the Wappinger Estuary.

After draining most of central and northern Dutchess County, Wappinger Creek, the major river of Dutchess County, roars through the village of Wappingers Falls over historic dams and past mills that once tapped the creek's enormous hydropower and gave the town its name. Just beyond the town, the creek falls to sea level and slams into the

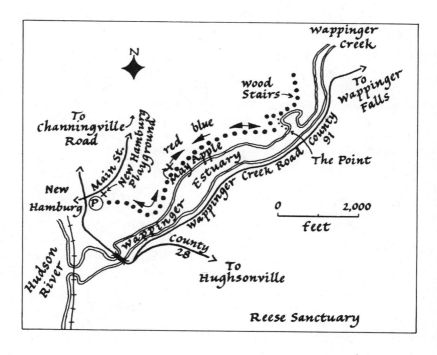

Hudson River. This happens a mile or so inland because the Hudson's tidal waters push all the way to the first waterfall of Wappinger Creek. The fresh inland waters of the Wappinger mix with the sometimes fresh, sometimes brackish Hudson waters to form the muddy churning soup of Wappinger Estuary.

ACCESS

From the light at the intersection of U.S. 9 and Dutchess County 28 (just south of the village of Wappingers Falls), turn west onto Dutchess County 28. Drive 1 mile to the light at Hughsonville. Go straight, still on Dutchess County 28/New Hamburg Road. Drive 1.2 miles. You will cross over the mouth of the Wappinger Estuary, with a view of the Hudson River and Central Hudson's plant at Danskammer Point. Upstream, you can see the creek's west bluff; that is Reese Sanctuary. At the next four-way intersection, you will be in the hamlet of New Hamburg. Turn right onto Main Street. Go 0.1 miles to New Hamburg Playground on your right. Park in the paved lot. Phone: the home of warden Michael Malone, (914) 297-3977. Early mornings are the best time to reach him.

TRAIL

After a long, cold winter of bleak trees, one yearns for the green leaves of summer. By the end of April, spring has finally come. Buds break open and woodland flowers bloom, but if you want a taste of summer weeks before it is due, visit Reese Sanctuary on a warm day during the first week in May.

Walk to the east end of the parking lot where a trail leads into the woods. What's this? The trees are leafed out! The forest floor is tall with green plants! How can this be?

Or come at the end of October. How can this be? Everywhere the trees are bare, but here autumn lingers and the trees are blazing yellow!

Former estate owners on the shores of the Hudson planted Norway maple (*Acer platanoides*) as an ornamental, but it escaped, spread, and outcompeted sugar maple (*Acer saccharum*, our official New York State tree) for sunlight, soil, and nutrients. The forested shorelands of the Wappinger area are dominated by Norway maple.

Norway maple leafs out far in advance of sugar or red maple, bringing summer to the forest floor weeks before normal. Cut a Norway maple leaf and out oozes milky sap. By late summer, the chlorophyll in the leaves of all the forest's trees is nearly exhausted. The fresh green of May and June changes to the duller tired green of August. Water availability in the ecosystem drops throughout the summer into the fall, and water will become totally unavailable when the ground freezes in December. Deciduous trees have no choice; they must shed their leaves to conserve water and survive.

In response to the decreasing sunlight, corky tissue forms between the leaf petiole and the twig, cutting off each leaf's sap supply. As it dies, the green chlorophyll breaks down to reveal yellow carotene pigments, present all along but masked by the chlorophyll. Red anthocyanin, another pigment, forms anew at this time, creating further color.

As with oaks and beeches, this corky tissue, or abscission layer, grows only partway on a Norway maple. All other trees' leaves will be down and the sky will be grey and cold, but the Norway maples will still display whole crowns of bright yellow leaves.

Spring and summmer come earlier and autumn lasts longer at Reese Sanctuary not only due to the presence of Norway maple, but also because of the moderating effect of the Hudson River on local air temperature.

What a delight to walk here the first week in May. The forest floor is thick with alien garlic mustard—tall, green, and already blooming. Follow the red trail. There are unmarked paths throughout this preserve. The red trail climbs the steep sand and clay bluff of Wappinger Creek. At the top, look back the way you came for a view through the trees of the Hudson River and New Hamburg. Continue on. There is a view of the Wappinger Estuary, unless the large Norway maple has already leafed out, in which case you'll get only a glimpse of water through an entire slope of summery green leaves. The spent yellow male flowers of the Norway maples lie on the ground. Migrating spring warblers sing, feed, and flit past the leaves.

Watch for the woodland plants that grow in moist, rich soils: yellow wood violet, fresh woodland ferns, carpets of trout lily, scores of Solomon's seal, and armies of Jack-in-the-pulpit. An old country trick (mostly among school boys) was to dig up a Jack-in-the-pulpit (*Arisaema atrorubens*) and dare a buddy to bite into the bulb-like corm. One crunch with the teeth, and the calcium oxalate crystals—a chemical commonly used to sandblast brick buildings—immediately sting the lips, mouth, and tongue with fire so acute that not even an hour of rinsing with water relieves the pain. Native People turned this

The garlic mustard is up and blooming and the trees are already leafed out.

poisonous plant edible. They dug up the corm, set it aside on a shelf to dry for one month, during which time the calcium oxalate crystals break down. This gave Jack-in-the-pulpit its other name of Indian turnip. Trudie Lamb-Richmond of the Schaghticoke Nation of Kent, Connecticut, says that a poultice of fresh Jack-in-the-pulpit berries on the skin is used to relieve the pain of arthritis and bursitis.

From here, near the creek's mouth, you can bushwhack to the shore of the estuary where you might see mating carp causing a rumpus in the weeds. Wappinger and Fishkill creeks are two of five major tributaries to the Hudson Estuary. Both form little estuary mouths onto the mother estuary of the Hudson, and are irreplaceable spawning spots for anadromous fishes, who spend their adult lives in the ocean and their young larval lives in the Hudson and the small estuaries of its tributaries. Between April and June alewife, blueback herring, white perch, and striped bass come to Wappinger Estuary to spawn. Soon after, they return to the ocean. The eggs hatch within several weeks and the estuary becomes a nursery. Tomcod swim into the estuary to spawn in December and January. Year-round freshwater residents include largemouth bass, bluegill, pumpkinseed, red-breasted sunfish, and brown bullhead.

The trail follows the bluff past Norway and sugar maple, red oak, hemlock, black birch, beech, a few tulip trees, and flowering dogwood. Several times the path crosses storm drainage systems for housing developments atop the bluff. In a few spots, storm water dumped into the beds of intermittent streams has caused stupendous erosion.

Near the first of these little canyons, the trail heads uphill through a vast patch of May apple (*Podophyllum peltatum*). When they first push up, May apple "heads" look like witch's spawn. The stalks shove higher to open into two leaf umbrellas on separate stalks. Between these stalks hangs the bud that opens into one waxy white flower. Its scent is nauseating. This ripens into the apple.

It is said that country children of the old days gathered these sweet, mawkish apples with addictive delight, and gorged themselves, unable to stop. Yet it is difficult to find these apples at their just-ripe stage. Eat one slightly unripe, and the podophyllin—made up of various acids and chemicals of which the worst for humans is podophyllo-quercetin—brings on a catharsis severe enough to cause hemorrhoids.

The trail follows up the estuary until it descends off the bluff, then back up wooden stairs to a view through the trees of the village of

Wild ginger.

Wappingers Falls. The estuary suddenly narrows to a creek, and the old mills come into sight. The trail ends. Turn around and, as you walk back, there is a view through the trees of the entire Beacon Range. Descend from the bluff, down the wooden stairs. At the bottom among the wild ginger, turn left onto the orange trail, a short path that leads to a point, a place to rest beside the water beneath hemlocks.

As with all major East Coast estuaries, the water of the Wappinger Estuary is muddy. But watch the water; you will see schools of Hudson River fish swim past, along with the familiar single sunfish of creek coves. Listen for the chirp of hunting osprey.

Return to the red trail that, on the return, becomes the blue trail. As you walk, there are a few views down the length of the estuary past the road bridge to the Hudson River.

The Hudson Highlands

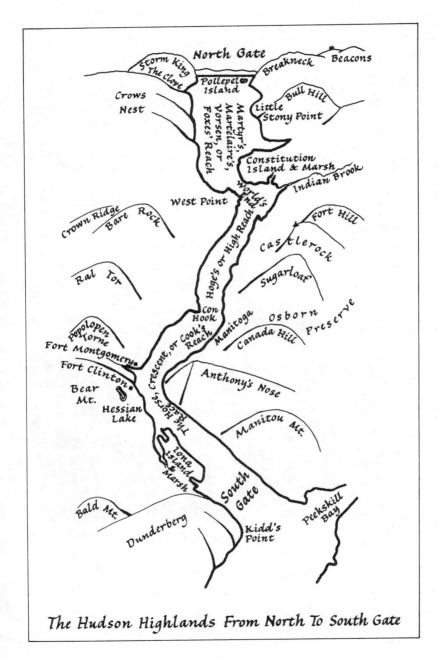

The Hudson Highlands From North To South Gate

Deepened by glaciers, the flooded Hudson river gorge is a true fjord—a tongue of the ocean reaching inland clear to Troy. For fifteen miles, the Hudson River breaches the Appalachian Mountains. From the North Gate at Storm King and Breakneck Ridge—truly a gate, the old Wey Gat or Wind Gate, where the river flows into a narrow gorge—to the South Gate at Dunderberg and Manitou Mountain, the river narrows and twists past the Hudson Highlands, the eroded roots of high mountains formed two hundred million years ago. *Wecquehacki*, the Lenape called these highlands, which in both Unami and Munsee translates as "end of the land."

What a remarkable river. An estuary, a gigantic riparian ecotone between salt- and freshwater and terrestrial habitats, rich, adorned with mountains. Enter through one of the gates in a sailing ship, and instantly feel the Highland's infamously treacherous winds. The Hudson runs at its deepest here, up to two hundred feet deep.

Ecologically, the Highlands are the heart of the Hudson Valley. Here is a major divide between northern and southern ecosystems of the eastern woodlands. North-facing slopes and shady ravines are suitable for northern birds such as Blackburnian warbler, Canada warbler, and brown creeper. Southern birds such as fish crow, cardinal, mockingbird, blue-grey gnatcatcher, tufted titmouse, and turkey vulture are near the northern limit of their ranges, as are opossum, fence lizard, and eastern mudminnow. Goshawk and golden-winged warbler, birds of the north, are near the southern limit of their ranges. Prickly pear cactus grow on dry sunny outcrops, while glacial relicts such as tundra bog moss and subarctic black spruce grow on top of the heights, at the southern limit of their ranges.

The river channel through the Highlands is deep and turbulent. Strong currents wash over the rocky bottom. This deep channel is the major spawning area for Hudson River striped bass. The only other such area on the east coast of the United States is in Chesapeake Bay. Half of the year, during spring and early summer, the Highlands stretch is freshwater. Come late summer, salt water intrudes in a wedge shape upstream. At different times of year one finds either freshwater, anadromous, or marine fishes, or all of them at once.

The Hudson River and its Highlands have been a catalyst, even a cause, of some of America's most important historical events. For 10,000 years, this wild, beautiful, bountiful land was the home of an indigenous people. The misunderstandings, intermarriages, and genocidal wars here between Natives and Europeans were typical of the early colonial period. This river and these hills were the geographical pivot of the American revolution. Almost one third of the American Revolutionary War battles were fought on or near the Hudson River. Inaccessible and stony, the Highlands were left unsettled for centuries while Europeans clear-cut the lowlands for agriculture.

Then came the industrial age. Mining and quarrying blasted Breakneck Ridge, Anthony's Nose, and Bull Hill. Railroads were built on *both* banks, cutting off the river from the people and the land. Storm King Highway was blasted into the face of Storm King Mountain.

The romantic era of the Hudson River School of painters and artists made the Highlands and the river famous throughout the world. Preservationists vied with industrialists. The American park and preservation movement began in the Hudson Valley with the crusade to save the Palisades from the quarrymen. That spark went on to inspire the national park system, the model for national parks around the globe. The battle to save Storm King from Consolidated Edison started the national environmental movement. And Clearwater's battle to save the Hudson River initiated America's search for clean water.

There are those residents who view the Hudson as an open sewer hopelessly contaminated with PCBs, used only by trains and ships. I sit at the river's edge in the town of Cold Spring and think how the river has gone the way of the Native People who once lived here. Misunderstood and taken advantage of, both lost to an aggressive and opportunistic people. Both forgotten.

But there is another view. The Hudson is guarded and triple-warded by a riverkeeper and numerous concerned governments and organizations who have banded together to form a Hudson Valley Greenway. The river is now busy with recreational boaters. And, on every weekend, the shoulders of NY 9D are lined with parked cars. Hikers go into the Hudson Highlands to explore and weave kinship with the landscape upon which they live.

31. Beacon Range

Location: Beacon
Distance: 8 miles; 8 to 10 hours
Owner: Private and posted, but open to hikers

North and south Beacon Mountains are the highest peaks between the Catskills and the Atlantic Ocean. The panoramic views from their summits are unparalleled. From the top of South Beacon one can see south to New York City and north to Albany, the *entire reach* of the tidal Hudson, east into Connecticut, again north to the Adirondacks, Vermont, and New Hampshire, and west to the Catskills.

According to legend, in 1682 Francis Rombout and Gulian Verplanck sealed a land deal on top of Mount Beacon with a group of Indians. The Natives had supposedly agreed to sell the pair "all the land they could see" on this side of the river. The view from on top of Mount Beacon cost the Natives 85,000 acres, and Rombout and Verplanck became known as shrewd businessmen. But David Oestreicher, a Lenape scholar, thinks that by 1682, most Natives in the area undoubtedly understood European land concepts and realized they were parting with their land forever. These Indians, greatly reduced in numbers by the ravages of European diseases, and feeling the pressure of their traditional hunting grounds being depleted, most likely found it difficult to hold onto large tracts of land. It made more sense at this point to sell the land and to emigrate. Of course, it wasn't always that way. At the very early phases of European-Native contact it is true there was little understanding from either party about the land concepts of the other. To Natives, land "sales" were merely leases for land use, sometimes quite specific (for example, for blackberry picking only), with the grantors always keeping the right to visit and likewise use the land as needed.

During the days of Rombout and Verplanck, the Beacon Mountains had a different name. The city of Beacon originally was known as Fishkill Landing, merely a river dock and depot for the important regional center of Fishkill. The mountains that run from Breakneck Ridge east to the Harlem Valley were named the Fishkill Range. The

169

most famous use of the Fishkill Range hills that shadow Fishkill Landing came during the revolution. Redoubts were kept on their summits as signal posts, beacons, visible for miles. The local militia was made up mostly of farmers' sons who, when things were peaceful, tended their farms, keeping an eye on the Fishkill Mountains for smoke by day and fire by night. Should the British sail up the Hudson, the ancient Celtic technique of communication throughout the realm was used: pyres were to be lit atop the North Redoubt, South Redoubt, and Mount Beacon, and the militia assembled. It is difficult to determine from the literature whether these beacons ever were actually lit, though it *is* known they were kept prepared and manned. As Fishkill Landing grew, it named itself after the mountain that looms over the city. Actually, there is a North Beacon Mountain and a South Beacon Mountain. North Beacon is the one with the antennas on its summit and is popularly known as Mount Beacon. For the sake of clarity, I'll call that part of the Fishkill Range from South Beacon to Bald Hill the Beacons.

This land is mostly privately owned, though open to hikers. The New York–New Jersey Trail Conference has blazed many trails through what is truly hikers' country. Trails climb straight up steep slopes. There are constant steep ups and downs. Since the range has been used for centuries, there are roads and trails everywhere, which makes it easy for the inexperienced to get disoriented. The trails often change, and trail conditions vary tremendously.

But the land is vast. Hudson Highlands State Park abuts South Beacon Mountain, and you could hike just these hills for a week. The Beacon Range is wild, lovely, and fragile. If I had to choose only one area in which to ramble, this would be it. Alas, it is not protected land.

ACCESS

Since this is private land, there exists no legal parking area, but the following has been used in the past. From the intersection of NY 9D and NY 52 in Beacon, proceed east/south on NY 9D. Cross Fishkill Creek and immediately bear left onto Spring Valley Road. Follow this into East Main Street, which will bear left and then right. Keep on this uphill until it becomes Mountain Avenue. At the fork with a yellow "No Outlet" sign, bear right on what appears to be an old

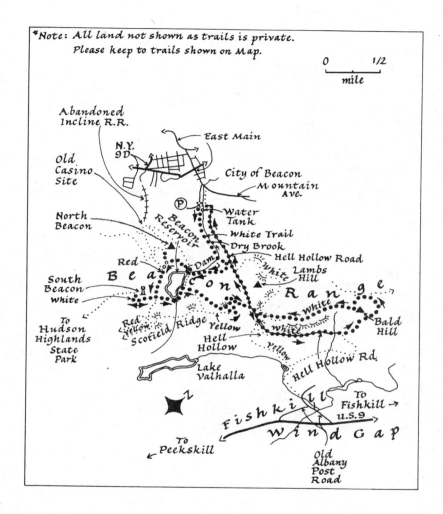

0   1/2

mile

Abandoned
Incline R.R.

East Main

N.Y.
9D

Old
Casino
Site

City of Beacon
Mountain
Ave.

Ⓟ

North
Beacon

Water
Tank

White Trail

Dry Brook

Hell Hollow Road

Lambs
Hill

Red

B e a c o n

R a n g e

South
Beacon
white

To
Hudson
Highlands
State
Park

Red

Scofield Ridge

Yellow

Hell
Hollow

white

Bald
Hill

Yellow

Hell Hollow Rd.

Lake
Valhalla

F i s h k i l l

To
Fishkill →
U.S.9

To
Peekskill

W i n d   G a p

Old
Albany
Post
Road

driveway, which will lead you to the Beacon water supply tank. Park in a pull-off *outside* the gate.

If there is no parking here, you'll have to go to the foot of the abandoned incline railway that climbs Mount Beacon and park there. Since the Beacon Range trails connect with Hudson Highlands State Park trails, you can also park along NY 9D in the pull-offs for Hudson Highlands State Park, but then we're talking a long hike.

TRAIL

Get a topographic map of the area: either the USGS West Point quadrangle or, better, the latest Beacon Range/Breakneck Ridge trail map number 11 of the east Hudson Trails published by the New York–New Jersey Trail Conference, available in bookstores.

Head up the paved road on the white trail beside the beautiful hemlock gorge of Dry Brook. The trail crosses the brook below a long waterfall that in winter becomes a long, white ice fall. Climb up a steep slope to the junction with the road that leads to Beacon Reservoir. In the 1930s, this was called Fishkill Reservoir. William Thompson Howell, Hudson Highlands photographer and writer in the early 1900s, described how it was newly formed by damming "one of the finest springs I ever knew" and flooding an abandoned farm and apple orchard. The white trail heads north to climb panoramic Lambs Hill. We head up the road to the reservoir.

Our goal is the fire tower on South Beacon Mountain, the highest mountain in the Highlands. There are several ways to get to it; take your pick. Personally, I can't resist going to the 1,531-foot peak of North Beacon (where the communications towers stand) for the view, especially at night when, as Howell wrote, Newburgh shimmers with lights like "stars below me in the darkness."

At the top of North Beacon is our first encounter with scrub oak (*Quercus ilicifolia*). Spiky, squat, and gnarled, scrub or bear oak grows no taller than a shrub, forming thickets. Bushwhack through this stuff and you'll get speared; the wood in those skinny branches is tough! Scrub and chestnut oaks, blueberry, mountain laurel, bracken fern, and an occasional pitch pine grow over the granite bedrock in a supremely xeric soil condition. The flora is adapted not only to this arid soil but also to storms and fires, which add up to one *rigorous* habitat.

Over the centuries, these mountaintop scrub oak habitats have seen little use, and probably look much as they did when Robert Juet looked at them from Henry Hudson's *Half Moon* on September 30, 1609, and wrote, "The Mountaynes looke as if some Metall or Minerall were in them. For the Trees that grow on them were all blasted, and some of them barren with few or no Trees on them."

You can walk down to the site of the casino where the incline railway once deposited fashionable gamblers. I hate to lose height once I've gained it, so I bushwhack to the red trail. From North Beacon, it can

On top of North Sugarloaf.

be seen (in winter, at least) leading up and towards South Beacon.

Why drive to the Berkshires or the Catskills for vast views of autumn color? Why spend hundreds of dollars to go to Canada for wilderness sights of rivers and hills? Come to the old New York State fire tower on South Beacon Mountain. Climb it, if you dare. Old isn't the word. Decrepit describes it better. But, compared to other old towers I've known, this one is strong and steady in the wind. The only problem is the missing planks on the stairs.

Even when they finally condemn it and take the tower away (may that day be far in the future, or—better yet—may they restore South Beacon tower and all towers with views for hikers), the panorama from 1,635-foot South Beacon will stay unrivaled. You can see New York City, the Catskills, Columbia County, and Connecticut. On a clear day the eastern United States stretches out before you: Vermont, New Hampshire, Massachusetts, Pennsylvania, the Adirondacks. Look how narrow Storm King really is, and the hemlocks that dot its north slope. Look how Crows Nest really is one broad mountain, the three peaks seen from the river only separate slopes. There's the hellish plant at Danskammer, puffing away. See the pink-yellow layer in the sky? Hudson Valley smog, much of it wafted on the wind upriver from New York City.

Cast about on the southeast side of the tower for the white trail. Take it north, back toward Beacon Reservoir. If you're feeling strong, take the yellow trail along Scofield Ridge. Otherwise, head down to Beacon Reservoir and take an unmarked road that leads northeast and looks at first like a wide, dry streambed. At the fork bear left. When you intersect the yellow trail, bear left onto a short steep white loop for the view. Continue on this white trail and it will rejoin the yellow trail.

Switchback down a steep hill to the valley and a road. Turn right, still on the yellow trail. Stay on the road, bearing right, past old stone walls. Who in their right mind would pick such a rocky mountain valley for a farm? Poor folk, likely. Farmers who could not afford the more expensive fertile land in the valley, or mountain men who wanted to be left to themselves. Farmers like J. P. Wood, Andrew Grier, L. Ackerman, and the Dingy families, who scratched out a living in the Beacons but whose farms did not last past the first generation.

You are walking on a road built before there were any farms, on what used to be known as an overmountain or notch road, in this case an east to west traversal of otherwise untraversable hills. Hell Hollow

Road has existed from at least 1858, and probably earlier. It connected Mountain Avenue with Albany Post Road (today's U.S. 9).

Hell Hollow Road brings you out to a view of what some say is the Fishkill Wind Gap. The north-facing slope of the hill opposite the trail is covered with hemlock. The hills plummet into Hell Hollow, a wild and windy drop choked with talus, best seen when the leaves are down. Head downhill, hugging the edge of the cliff. Watch on the left for the white trail, still Hell Hollow Road. Take it.

What's the Fishkill Wind Gap? See U.S. 9 below in the wide valley? Once, a river flowed there, and eroded the valley cutting *across* the grain of the hills, forming a water gap. Most rivers and streams erode *along* the flanks of hills, *with* the grain. The Highland gorge of today's Hudson River is a water gap, cutting across the grain of the Appalachians. When a river abandons such a cross-grain valley through high hills, the water gap becomes a wind gap. Some folks theorize that this valley may simply be erosion along a fault.

Hell Hollow Road stays level for a good distance. After it crosses a stream, the road curves downhill to Albany Post Road (U.S. 9) while our white trail begins the ascent up Bald Hill. Stay on the white trail. At the summit, the view is obscured by trees. Follow the white trail, and now, *there's* a view! The Hudson winds south clear to the Atlantic through peaks as jagged and glorious as views I've seen out west in the Rockies. The white trail wends along rock outcrops until it intersects Hell Hollow Road. Keep straight for Lambs Hill, if you prefer. More likely, it's getting late. Head home along Hell Hollow Road, downhill through the Dry Brook valley to Mountain Avenue.

There are plenty of other walks in the Beacon Range. The top of North Sugarloaf has the best views of the Bannerman castle ruins on Pollepel Island. There are also two of those blasted trees we're always hearing about in the romantic literature and seeing in those Hudson River School paintings. Perhaps the finest full-day hike in the Highlands would be to climb the spectacular open ridge of Breakneck to South Beacon Mountain, tramp clear to Bald Hill, returning over North Sugarloaf. Melzingah Hollow and the Wilkinson Memorial Trail lead through beautiful areas. There are so many unmarked roads that, truly, the area is a hiker's paradise and should become one contiguous protected park.

32. Bull Hill, Hudson Highlands State Park

Location: Cold Spring
Distance: 6 miles; 7 to 8 hours
Owner: State of New York

What do the Brooklyn Bridge, West Point, the Taconic State Parkway, NY 44, the old IBM in Beacon, and the front steps of the capital building in Albany have in common? They are all built of granite blasted from Bull Hill and Breakneck Ridge.

A man named Southard wanted to be rid of Bull Hill. Property taxes for the south slope of an entire mountain were high, especially a mountain as wide as old Bull Hill. He offered the land to New York State as a park, but the state dragged its feet and did nothing. So, Southard put Bull Hill and Little Stony Point on the commercial market. The Hudson River Stone Corporation of New York City bought the property in 1931. They immediately set up crusher operations, and the public immediately protested.

After a long public battle, the quarry on Bull Hill and Little Stony Point was finally closed in 1966. Only a year later, when the public thought the place safe, Georgia Pacific Corporation applied for a license to build an eight million dollar plasterboard plant on Little Stony Point. Under pressure, New York State snatched the Point from harm's way. In 1968, with matching private and state funds, the Taconic State Park Commission purchased Bull Hill, North Sugarloaf, Pollepel Island, and what they didn't already own of Breakneck Ridge to form Hudson Highlands State Park.

Some say protection came too late for Bull Hill, scarred beyond repair. As for Breakneck, its face had been blasted for decades during the 1800s. Little Stony Point had its head blown off. Bannerman's Castle on Pollepel Island blew up and burned on its own. Other than North Sugarloaf, the area was far from pristine.

We will not avoid these scars as we hike. We will go and look at them. They remind us that the precious Hudson Valley landscape is never safe unless vigilantly guarded. They remind us that damage done can be damage done forever.

Despite the abuses they have suffered, Little Stony Point and Bull Hill are beautiful places. You must go see them.

ACCESS

Park in the pull-offs along NY 9D beside Little Stony Point. This is just north of Cold Spring and the intersection of NY 9D and Fair Street. Phone: Fahnestock State Park office, (914) 225-7207.

TRAIL

Little Stony Point is a joy. Despite the years of blasting that removed its impressive granite cliffs, it contains the finest river views on the Hudson's east bank and the Hudson's best sand beach.

Cross the railroad bridge that leads to Little Stony Point and turn right for a short loop. There's Sandy Beach, a popular spot for boaters, picnickers, and sunbathers. Bring wieners and have a barbecue. (If you were turn-of-the-century photographer and writer William Thompson Howell, you'd bring steaks, a pair of capons, wine, and cigars. But you wouldn't cook them on Sandy Beach. You'd carry them with your broiler on a bushwhack in the middle of winter to the top of Bull Hill and feast while you admired the view.)

The path brings you past the remnants of Little Stony Point's cliffs (on your left). Feel the wind? That is the infamous Highland wind historically treacherous to sailboats. It barrels down from The Clove, also known as Mother Cronk's Cove, the valley between Storm King and Crows Nest. Upriver stands the North Gate: Storm King to the west, Breakneck to the east, Pollepel Island in the center. Overhead towers Crows Nest. And there is Bull Hill, and the quarry scar. We're going *all* the way up there?

At this northwest tip of Little Stony Point the water is 140 feet deep. The barges were moored here at a dock and loaded with crushed mountain rock.

Continue around the point. On the south side, there is an old mine tunnel from the iron-ore days of the early 1800s. Crouch and crawl in. The level tube curves into pitch blackness; you'll need a flashlight to find the T intersection.

Cross back over the railroad tracks and head north on NY 9D. The grassy, white trail climbs steeply up the bank, following the site of

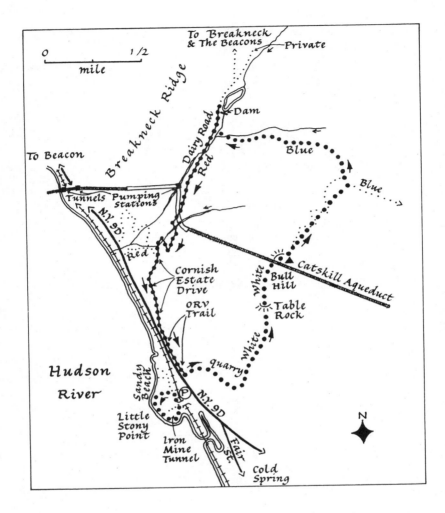

the crusher tipple: huge rock processing buildings and chutes on stilts that extended from the quarry to the river "like steps in the hillside."

Emerge out into the amphitheater of the quarry. Take a walk around the loop at the base. It looks like the African savanna. Fire could have done this, or the characteristic black locust has of forming colonies connected underground, but my guess is that the compacted, sunlit, dry soil has caused the locust trees among the grasses to be evenly spaced from one another. This avoids intense competition for the scant supply of water. Such spacing is commonly found in dry desert eco-systems in the western United States.

Return to the white trail, which follows up the south lip of the quarry. The climb is steep. The oaks are short and stunted. When the trees are bare, you get views, but none of them compare to the open view from Table Rock: West Point, Constitution Island and Marsh, Sugarloaf, Crows Nest, Storm King, and Breakneck. Continue. You'll crest the mountain, but there will be no view until you reach the old carriage road. The slope of Bull Hill falls away at your feet into the Lake Surprise valley, and rolls up onto Breakneck Ridge. This would be where William Thompson Howell would break out that broiler and cook his chops.

Imagine, one thousand feet beneath your feet, through the heart of Bull Hill inside a fourteen-foot diameter tube, the finest public drinking water in America courses through the Catskill Aqueduct headed for the faucets of New York City. Five hundred million gallons a day, and it's not enough.

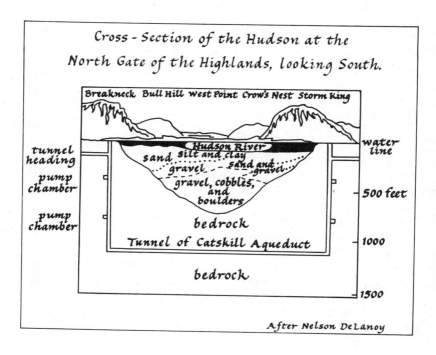

Cross - Section of the Hudson at the North Gate of the Highlands, looking South.

After Nelson DeLanoy

Right around here somewhere in the early 1700s a wild bull caroused the countryside, ravaging nearby farms when hungry, threatening woodcutters and hunters. The farmers decided it had to go. A posse on horseback with dogs hunted up the slopes of the bull's hill and chased the renegade clear down Lake Surprise ravine and up the other side to the very edge of the cliff. The bull fell off, breaking its neck, hence: Breakneck Ridge and Bull Hill. During the romantic years of the 1800s, an attempt was made to Victorianize the "coarse" name Bull Hill into Mount Taurus, as was done to Butter Hill, which became Storm King, and Crows Nest, which became Cro' Nest.

Continue on the white trail. Notice how the oak and laurel woods on the right side of the path were burned. Nearly every summer, especially in drought years, the media tells the public of forest fires, caused by lightning or human carelessness, burning out of control on Bull Hill, Breakneck, or in the Beacons. These fires sweep over the hills, sometimes scorching hundreds of acres before bush firefighters squelch them. Such fires tend to kill young hemlock, young white pine, maple, and beech stems. This reduces competition for the more fire-resistant oaks and hickories. Centuries of this, coupled with the xeric conditions of hilltops and historical woodcutting, has led to the scrub- and chestnut-oak-dominant forests we see on the summits of the Highlands. From journals of the earliest explorers, it seems these scrubby, fire-resistant forests have been on these summits for a long time.

To descend, take the steep blue trail north into the Lake Surprise/Breakneck Brook valley. At the dirt road, turn right. Look at the spooky old buildings! You are on the original road that connected Beacon to Cold Spring, the old Lake Surprise Road that became Dairy Road when Edward G. Cornish built his estate.

Chairman of the board of the National Lead Company, Mr. Cornish could afford the best. His early 1900 estate was large. Walk up the road, past his farm. The barn ruin has some of the fanciest stone- and brickwork I've ever seen devoted to cows. I have never known cows to need fires to keep warm, yet this barn has a chimney, and the barn was partially heated. There are abandoned barns, sheds, garages, a pasteurizing house, coops, lofts, and, at the concrete dam and pond, a ruined two-story wood-frame tenant house. Notice how the dam (Mr. Cornish's last project) is in perfect condition.

Return back down Dairy Road, where it becomes the red trail. You'll pass a round concrete cistern large enough to be a swimming pool. The tall wooden tube inside still contains some of the charcoal used to filter the drinking water from Breakneck Brook. Pass the shell of the greenhouse, the large swimming pool, the formal gardens, and, lastly, the ruins of the mansion. Built from rocks hewn from Breakneck Mountain, the house contained the luxury of indoor plumbing.

The red trail becomes a concrete road with hardly a pothole or a crack. How many *new* paved or concrete roads do you know that look so good? Mildred Eaton Carr, daughter of builder James W. Eaton, recalled how the very best of materials was used in building the estate, which is why things have lasted. The elder Cornishes died during the 1930s. Pending property settlement, the farm was boarded up and left vacant. The house burned in 1956, probably from careless campers.

A sidetrail takes you to a large stone building with a sign, "Erected AD 1913." This is a pumphouse for the Catskill Aqueduct, which originates in Ashokan Reservoir and, incredibly, passes *beneath* the Hudson River. Engineers drilled for four years through layer upon layer of silt, sand, gravel, and boulders, seeking the bottom of the Hudson at Storm King. Endless, they thought, bottomless; the gorge was choked with glacial debris. At 1,114 feet below the river surface, their angled east and west diamond drill borings met in solid rock. The original bed of the Hudson gorge is deeper than the Hudson Highland mountains are high.

Follow Dairy Road. Just before the gate at NY 9D, turn left. Off-road vehicles have trampled a trail that will return you to the white trail where it began off NY 9D.

33. Constitution Marsh Sanctuary

Location: Garrison
Distance: Less than 1 mile; 2 to 3 hours
Owner: New York State, managed by National Audubon
Society

There are two parcels to Constitution Marsh Sanctuary: the marsh itself, and the Indian Brook ravine. The visit to each is one-way, so you may either first walk uphill to see the ravine and the waterfalls, or downhill to the Hudson for the boardwalk through the cattails.

ACCESS

From U.S. 9D, south of Cold Spring and just south of Boscobel Restoration (a place to visit after you walk), turn west onto Indian Brook Road. Drive 0.5 miles to the sanctuary sign. No pets allowed. The trails are open every day from 8 AM to 6 PM. Phone: sanctuary manager, (914) 265-3119.

TRAIL

Henry Hudson did not get on well with some of the Native People who lived along the river that today bears his name. He sailed north to the future site of Albany, and by the time he returned to New York Harbor, he'd killed, for various reasons, fourteen or so Native People. The Natives weren't happy about this. On Hudson's trip downriver, he anchored in Newburgh Bay for two foggy days. An unarmed party of sailors went ashore near Glenham. They were attacked by Indians, an undocumented but persistent local tale says, and Jacobus Van Horen was wounded and captured while the rest fled back to the *Half Moon.*

Van Horen was taken into the hills around Matteawan, today's Beacon Range, and we cringe to think what his captors contemplated. Princess Manteo, daughter of the chief, saw the captive, fell in love with him, and pleaded for the white man's life. He was given to her, their marriage planned for a year hence. An excellent fisherman, Jacobus was allowed to roam freely in the Indian Brook area, each day bringing in a supply of trout.

But one day, when they were swimming in the pool below Indian Brook Falls (a spot still popular with young lovers), Henry Hudson's man spotted a European ship on the river. Jacobus abandoned Manteo and bolted for the shore. He was seen and picked up. Manteo's body was found in the pool. Some say Jacobus murdered her to escape. Others say that after her lover fled, Manteo walked broken-hearted and weeping up Indian Brook, a white flower springing up where each tear fell to earth. At the falls, she hurled herself from the clifftop to her death in the pool.

Now you know why it's called Indian Brook.

This tale, while totally European in origin, does give insight into the numerous misunderstandings and intermarriages typical of the early contact between Europeans and Natives.

From your car, go up the narrow dirt Indian Brook Road along the

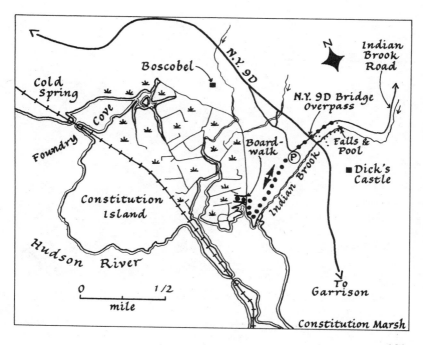

top of the ravine. Pass beneath the NY 9D bridge. When Indian Brook Road turns sharply right, there is a rough path that plummets down to Indian Brook Falls. You can glimpse the foam through the leaves. The young and famous actress Fanny Kemble likewise so glimpsed the foam in 1833, and it made her "wild to go down." When you go down to the foot of the falls and the pool, do not feel as Miss Kemble did: "an uncontrollable desire seized me to clamber up the rocks by the side of the fall, and so reach the top of it." She nearly killed herself and the man helping her. Indian Brook Falls for a time was known as Fanny Kemble's Bath.

Return back down the road to your car. Continue on the dirt road that follows the top of the ravine wall of Indian Brook, going steeply downstream. The road is lined with paving stones, remnants of the homesite that we find at the road's end, along with Norway spruce trees planted by the owner.

Signs point the way to the boardwalk. Cross the lawn of the new nature center, built with a grant from the Hudson River Improvement Fund. (This fund is a $3 million settlement made three years ago by the Exxon Corporation as part of a lawsuit filed by the Hudson River Fishermen's Association. Exxon was sued for taking fresh Hudson River water and selling it in the Caribbean.)

Cattails in the wind. In the background are Bull Hill to the right and Storm King and Crows Nest on the left.

Green-twigged cat brier (*Smilax rotundifolia*) twines by its tendrils and drapes the woods in a tangle beloved by small birds. Birds sleekly slip through the mazed fortress that no large predator can penetrate. Hooked, sharper than the claws of cats, the thorns of the cat brier are the most vicious the hiker can encounter. They are strong, and tear not only clothing, but flesh, too. The male and female vines are separate, one bearing pollen, the other eggs in green flowers that ripen into blue-black berries, also beloved by birds. The round leaves with their parallel veins often remain green far into autumn. In protected spots, they grow evergreen.

At junctions with side trails, keep straight. The first indication that you are nearing the marsh is a swamp of red maple, tupelo, alder, and ostrich fern. In spring and fall, color shows first in swamps. It is here that skunk cabbages bloom, often before the snow has melted, and it is here that the red maples fuzz out red and orange in April, while the hills are still stark and cold. As early as late August, the red maple leaves begin to turn scarlet. And nowhere are the fall colors more vibrant than in October when the sun shines upon an entire swamp of red maple saplings colored in brilliant red, orange, and yellow.

As you walk west, the tree and shrub height lowers. Cattail and loosestrife grow among the alder. Then the woody plants end, and it's all cattail marsh. This progression, red maple swamp to cattail marsh, is typical and corresponds to increasing soil moisture that leads to arrowhead, arrow arum, and pickerelweed, then open water.

Follow the bedrock of the bluff edge past cushions of moss and chestnut oak. The trail turns right uphill. Pitch pine grows on the top. It is amazing how a bone-dry plant community lies adjacent to a sopping wet one, the line between them no thicker than a trail. Water rules plant species. In ecological terminology, water is a limiting factor. Corresponding to this difference in plant habitats are different associated animal species.

The view from the top of the bluff shows a piece of marsh, the Hudson, West Point, and mountains south. Continue on to the boardwalk, 300 feet long, an observation blind at its end. There are views downriver of Anthony's Nose, The Timp, and Bear Mountain bridge. To the west is Constitution Island, for which the marsh is named, Storm King, and the south crown of Crows Nest. To the north looms Bull Hill.

Constitution Marsh is a tidal freshwater/brackish marsh of 270 acres.

It is one of the largest undeveloped tidal wetlands on the Hudson River, supporting an unusual diversity and abundance of wildlife species. In late summer, the Atlantic salt front moves upstream past the marsh and one can find blue crab and shrimp among the cattails. Any time of year, this is a fantastic place for bird watching, though not at any time of day. Many birds are crepuscular, active at dawn and dusk. If you come here at noon, the place may seem dead.

Even during the day, spring and fall migration participants of up to 200 species wing through in fantastic flocks. Can you imagine seeing wood ducks by the hundreds? Thirty-one species of birds use the marsh for breeding. In late summer, there are the hordes of swallows at dusk. In winter, there are usually bald eagles. In summer, the most common nesting bird is the marsh wren. But the red-winged blackbirds are the noisiest.

Our first bird of spring, the male red-wings return from the southern states up the ancient flypath of the Hudson River in middle to late February. On the first warm day of March, they disperse inland to the marshes of Dutchess and Putnam counties. They settle in among the brown cattail leaves to battle for nesting sites, using song and occasional ritualistic sparring as weapons. Two or three weeks later the brown females fly north to select the mates of their choice and raise their broods. The nests are built of cattail fibers that are attached to the stalks. The males perch upon the dipping cattail leaves, sing their territorial boundaries, and pluck insects off the cattail stems for their nestlings.

Red-wings and cattails go together.

In 1837, Henry Warner, owner and resident of Constitution Island, decided to grow wild rice. He diked Constitution Marsh and dug the channels still visible today. In 1851, the railroad was built. In 1952, the U.S. Army Corps of Engineers built a factory at Cold Spring to produce rechargeable nickel-cadmium batteries. Under successive owners, the plant operated until 1979, polluting Foundry Cove with cadmium, nickel, and cobalt so badly that the area is listed as one of the most serious hazardous waste sites in the United States of America and one of the largest and most concentrated cadmium-contaminated sites in the world.

Dumped into Foundry Cove were about twenty-five metric tons of cadmium. The heavy metal element sank to the muck, where it was picked up by cattails and other plants at such an incredible rate that sampled cattail roots were found in 1977 to contain up to 72.3 parts per million (ppm) of cadmium. For comparison, control cattails sampled at Black Creek Marsh in Albany County contained 0.13 ppm cadmium. Near the factory's discharge pipe, the cove sediment was found to contain 171,000 ppm cadmium. Any animal that eats Foundry Cove cattail roots, or shoots, or leaves, accumulates the heavy metal in its body. The result depends on the amount ingested: outright death, reproductive failure, or disease.

Every organism of this marsh contains cadmium, not only plants but crabs, snapping turtles, muskrats, and fish. Constitution Marsh, as with all marshes, has functioned as a giant sink or sponge and held the deadly cadmium, nickel, and cobalt in place, preventing them from getting into the main flow of the Hudson River and into our drinking water.

But the cadmium doesn't stop there totally. A tidal marsh produces ten to fifteen tons of biomass per acre per year, as compared to our best farmland which produces a paltry two to five tons per year at a greater cost in equipment, fertilizer, pesticides, and storage. A tidal marsh is the most productive of places. When the biomass of tidal marsh cattails and plants dies, it decays into detritus, the basis for fisheries that produce millions of fish per acre. Tidal marshes, Constitution Marsh among them, are *the* spawning and feeding grounds for perhaps eighty percent of all the species of Atlantic Ocean fish and shellfish.

Fifty million federal dollars have been allocated to clean up Constitution Marsh and Foundry Cove and take the cadmium, nickel, and cobalt elsewhere. (Where is a "safe place" for such toxins?) Forty acres of Foundry Cove will be excavated. The New York State–owned marsh, though it contains hot spots of the heavy metals, will not be touched. If these hot spots were removed, then alien purple loosestrife and phragmites would enter, outcompete, and replace the cattail. The entire marsh flora and fauna would change.

The current slides beneath the boardwalk. Wind rustles the cattails, and the red-wings smack and trill. A buoy bell tolls in the river channel while an osprey hunts Hudson River fish grown in Foundry Cove.

By the view, you'd never know the poison was there.

But it's a common waste. Cadmium is used to make rubber tires, alloys, plastics, pigments, plated wares, insecticides, paints, solar cells, solders, and cigarettes. Ward Stone, of New York State's Department of Environmental Conservation Department, has asked, how many other Foundry Coves are out there?

34. Castle Rock Unique Area

Location: Garrison
Distance: 3.25 miles; 3 hours
Owner: State of New York

Have you ever driven along NY 9D just south of Garrison and seen a castle way up on a hill? I mean a real fairy-tale castle with stone turret, narrow windows, slanting red roofs, and tall rooms, all high atop a hill. That's Castle Rock.

Built by William Henry Osborn, president of Illinois Central Railroad, in 1881 when medieval castles were the rage of the Hudson Valley elite, Castlerock (the name for the house itself is one word) overlooks the Hudson Highlands as a lord would over his fiefdom.

Five generations of Osborns have lived at the thirty-four room mansion, the focal point of the 2,500-acre estate. In the 1970s, the property was offered in parcels on the real estate market. The contents of the mansion were auctioned off in a weekend extravaganza remembered by many locals. Before his death, Beatle singer John Lennon considered buying the castle for his home. New York State expressed interest, but in the end, the mansion itself remained in Osborn family hands, while the state obtained the bulk of the properties. Castle Rock Unique Area is a small portion of what the state acquired, the rest being the Osborn Preserve or Sugarloaf/Canada Hill portion of Hudson Highlands State Park. Castle Rock Unique Area includes fields, hemlock woods, and steep slopes.

The trick at Castle Rock is to keep on state land without trespassing onto private property. To connect trails, you would at times need to bushwhack. None of the trails are marked. Most are old carriage roads. Seldom used, some are difficult to see. It is longer but easier to follow trails onto the Osborn section of Hudson Highlands State Park and then swing back into Castle Rock to visit Lake Elizabeth.

ACCESS

Just south of the intersection of NY 9D and NY 403 is Highland

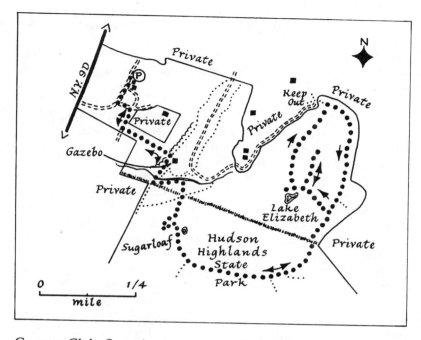

Country Club. Opposite the green are fields. You can see the castle up there on the ridge. Watch the stone wall that lines the east side of the highway for two stone pillars. The right pillar says "Wing & Wing 1857." This name comes from the original farmhouse on the estate William Osborn bought in 1855, which was enlarged with additions many times. The left pillar says "Castlerock 1881." Drive through the pillars and park at the designated area by the barns. Phone: New York State Department of Environmental Conservation office at Stony Kill Farm, (914) 831-3109.

TRAIL

Walk back the way you drove. Just past the barn where you parked is a driveway. Do not follow it. Keep walking and take the next driveway on your left. Do not follow this all the way to the house. Instead, take the first right that leads through the fields, paralleling NY 9D, then take the first left that heads straight to the forested hill with the castle. You will know you have found the right place when you enter woods and spot an old cedar-wood gazebo. The gazebo's railings and

189

posts were intricately carved by bark beetle larvae who hatched from eggs under the bark of the live cedar tree, then tunneled and ate. Once old enough, they pupated into adult beetles and emerged into the light of day, leaving their carvings behind, hidden, until the tree was chopped down and hammered into a gazebo.

From this spot you see a huge view upriver of the gray towers and turrets of West Point and the notch behind where the Hudson River flows. This trail is held in place by a stone retaining wall on its downhill side, unremarkable at first but gradually gaining in height and importance. It is hard work to cut a trail into a slope and build such a wall. If you bushwhack around this forest you will run across much work such as this along the way. Another retaining wall can be seen uphill through the trees. That road is private, and leads to the castle. We may cross this castle road, but, as the state puts it, "pedestrian or vehicular access along the road" is forbidden. Please respect the privacy of residents and do not trespass on private property. Any time you see a lawn you are looking at private property.

Head south on this old carriage trail. Just beyond the gazebo, when the trail begins a downslope, watch for a deer crossing. A narrow trail, well defined, cuts perpendicular to our trail. Just beyond it cuts another. Creatures of habit, deer. That's why one sees "deer crossing" signs on roads. Once a trail is made, countless successive generations of deer use that trail.

Cross an intermittent stream and stop at the stone wall. Ahead lies Sugarloaf Mountain and the property of Osborne Preserve of Hudson Highlands State Park. Turn left uphill. Switchback up and up through the hemlocks. At the fork head straight through the stone wall and take the left fork on the other side.

This carriage path takes you up and along the northeast slope of Sugarloaf Mountain. Pass a small wetland on your left. At the intersection turn left, continuing up a wooded valley, passing another small wetland and then a pond—both this time on your right. Keep straight past all intersections, bearing left twice more as you climb. The trail will level out for a while and you will arrive at a third intersection. Turn left.

Watch for a path on your right that leads to the top of the mountain. Dry, resinous white pines grow here and through the trees is a view. Explore the remains of a cabin. Return back down and turn right to visit Lake Elizabeth.

At the beach, hundreds of frogs and tadpoles flee your approach, darting under the water milfoil. This is a man-made pond; see the cement dam? It's a pretty, peaceful place, quiet, ringed with hemlock, oak, red maple, and black birch. Sedges stand in the shallows.

To follow the trails at the top of the hill is a breeze. Return the way you came and take the first left to circle the ridge. The walk stays level through hemlocks atop steep ravine wall drops. Keep right at the next junction and you'll find yourself back at the trail for home. Turn left to retrace your steps to your car.

The wooded trail at Castle Rock.

35. Osborn Preserve, Hudson Highlands State Park

Location: Garrison
Distance: 7 miles; 3 to 5 hours
Owner: State of New York

Osborn Preserve, when combined with Castle Rock Unique Natural Area and National Park Service land along the Appalachian Trail, totals 1,500 acres. Trails also link these properties to Manitoga Preserve. Osborn Preserve was donated by the Osborn family to New York State in 1974. It lies in the heart of the Hudson Highlands, rich in colonial and Revolutionary War history, and a joy to explore. In 1778, Dr. Dwight, a chaplain of a Connecticut regiment stationed at West Point, described the view from Sugarloaf Mountain as: "majestic, solemn, wild, and melancholy."

ACCESS

There is no developed parking area for the Osborn Preserve, but you can find a spot for your car at the intersection of US 9 and NY 403 near Graymoor. There's some space along the road, a vacant lot, a gas station, and some vacant stores. Pick what seems best. As part of Hudson Highlands State Park, Osborn Preserve is under the jurisdiction of the Taconic region of the New York State Office of Parks, Recreation, and Historic Preservation. Phone: Fahnestock State Park office, (914) 225-7207 or the regional office in Staatsburg, (914) 889-4100.

TRAIL

Find the vertical white rectangle blaze of the Appalachian Trail (AT) on the west side of the highway intersection. The trail heads across a

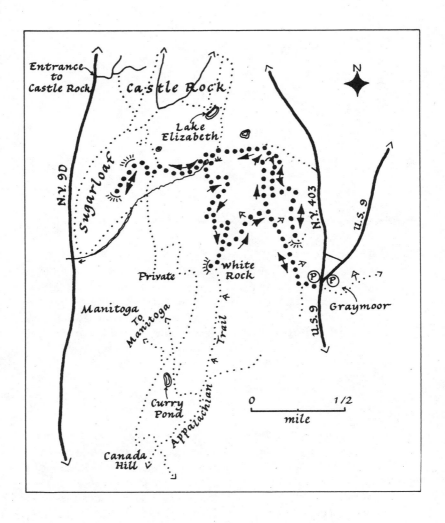

wet meadow atop wood planks. At the woods, keep on the AT, an old carriage road that soon leads into mountain laurel, oak, and sassafras. The trail follows up a brook valley. Brilliant yellow tulip tree leaves shine against the blue sky of autumn. The AT turns left to climb the valley wall. We keep straight.

The brook widens into a small swampy area, what early Dutch colonists called a *vly*. A brook was called a *kil*. This *vly* is the *kil's* headwaters, where the water table first surfaces. The trail climbs to a high point, and then starts—ever so slightly—downhill. On the opposite side of the path is another *vly*, and from it runs another *kil*, but in the opposite direction from the last. You have just crossed a watershed line, or divide, the ridge that separates two different drainage basins. These two brooks, their headwaters mere meters apart, flow in opposite directions. Each ravine funnels all its water into the brook that drains it.

The water from both these brooks eventually drains into the Hudson, placing them within the Hudson River watershed. Most of Putnam and Dutchess counties are within the Hudson River watershed. A small portion to the east lies within the Housatonic watershed. The continental divide of the Rocky Mountains separates the United States into Atlantic and Pacific ocean watersheds. There is a mountain in Glacier National Park, Montana, called Triple Divide. From this peak water flows into three watersheds: the Atlantic, the Pacific, and Hudson's Bay. When one considers development decisions for the Hudson River, it is not enough to look only at the river. One must include the entire Hudson River watershed: 14,000 square miles. It is the entire drainage basin that makes up the Hudson, not just the water body itself.

Enter a hemlock woods. Watch carefully for a trail on the right. This is a one-way sidetrip that ascends a hill and affords a view on a clear day of the Hudson south to the Empire State Building and the World Trade Towers. See them, the skyscrapers, behind the hills? Mere little needles.

Return to the trail at the base of the hill. Continue, bearing left at the four-way intersection, left again at the three-way intersection, and then left at the next junction. Royal fern grows lushly in a *vly*. Continue straight past striped maples.

The trail heads downhill alongside a brook. The brook tumbles down a steep incline, while the trail follows at a gentler grade above tall retaining walls. At a tight curve sits an old gazebo of cedar, the twin of the one at Castle Rock, right down to its bark-beetle carvings. At the bottom of the ravine, find the thin path that steeply climbs Sugarloaf Mountain. The first view from the top is of Bull Hill, Breakneck, Little Stony Point, Newburgh, Storm King, Crows Nest, the Shawangunks, Constitution Island, West Point, and the sharp bend of the Hudson River called World's End. The plan was for this sharp bend to slow down British war ships so that they couldn't break the second Great Chain, a chain of huge iron links on a floating boom of logs, which stretched from Constitution Island to West Point from 1778 to the end of the Revolutionary War. Trapped, the ships could then be destroyed by cannon. The chain was never put to the test, unlike the first Great Chain at Anthony's Nose. After their defeat at Saratoga, the British did not try the Highlands again.

The footpath continues along the narrow arête-like crest. If looked at from the south by someone coming upriver in a boat, Sugarloaf is a perfect pyramid, just like an old-fashioned loaf of sugar, a *suycker broodt*, hung by a string in the center of Dutch tables. It was on Sugarloaf that one of the many Hudson River Revolutionary War cannon redoubts were kept. General Israel Putnam's men evidently became bored when the British stayed away. One day they rolled a boulder off the top of Sugarloaf and with glee watched it crash down the mountain, crushing huge trees. They claimed it landed in the river, and they named it for their general, who, it is said, jumped on top of it and proclaimed it rightful American territory.

As a ledge comes in sight, on your left you'll see—could it be?—cactus. It is prickly pear cactus (*Opuntia humifusa*), with showy yellow flowers, maroon fruits, and protective spines. The only cactus found in the East occurs along the Hudson River on warm, exposed rocky and sandy sites. Normally, prickly pear is a coastal plain plant, where it grows in dry sunny habitats. The Hudson River, as an extension of the ocean, mediates the local climate. As a trough, the river allows warm air to funnel inland. This allows coastal and southern species access to the Highlands, not only prickly pear cactus but also fence lizard and Carolina wren.

The ledge. The view. The Hudson spread wide below. There's Anthony's Nose, Bear Mountain, and Bear Mountain Bridge spanning the chasm between.

As you return along the ridge, note the privet bushes and the arrowwood. These and others seem to be signs that the top of Sugarloaf was once an open field. Indeed, early writings state that the Beverly Robinson house at the north foot of Sugarloaf was visible from the summit. Beverly was the manor house for a 60,000-acre Tory estate that was confiscated and used as a busy rebel headquarters by Washington, Lafayette, Hamilton, and Benedict Arnold. That house saw a lot of history. Arnold lived here, and it was in this house that he was to meet and to have breakfast with General Washington. Instead, upon receiving news that British Major John André had been captured

On top of Sugarloaf looking south down the Hudson River to Anthony's Nose and Bear Mountain.

carrying the plans for West Point in his boot, Arnold fled and defected to the British.

As you walk further, note how the cooler, moister northwest river-facing slope is all grown in hemlock, while the warmer southeast inland-facing slope is all deciduous. Like a line down the mountain side, the annual mean microclimate changes, and likewise does the climax vegetation.

At the base of Sugarloaf, return up the ravine and turn right at the intersection. Climb until the junction with the AT. Just beyond, watch on your right for a blue side trail that leads to White Rock and another view from Anthony's Nose clear to the Shawangunks. There's Sugarloaf, a shorter mountain than the one on which we stand. Now you can really see its sugar-loaf cone shape.

Backtrack and take the AT downhill, turn right at the carriage road, and retrace to your car.

36. Manitoga

Location: Garrison
Distance: 1.5 miles; 1 to 2 hours
Owner: Manitoga, Inc.

After a successful career in industrial design, Russel Wright purchased nearly eighty acres near Manitou, where he built a country home for himself and his family. In addition to being used for timber, the land had been quarried, and was scarred with pits and holes. To an artist and a designer, to heal such damaged land was a challenge. Wright studied the site and noted the themes of biological structure, processes, ecology, and human land use. Then, for thirty years he sculpted a forest garden. He landscaped and reclaimed the land to create what he considered the crowning achievement of his famous career.

Manitoga is a Mahican word that probably means "spirit ground." The name is derived from the word *manitou*, which means "spirit" or "deity" in the Mahican and Lenape languages, and *kai* or "ground" in Mahican. *Manitou* is a catchall phrase loosely and variously applied to many religious things, or to the spiritual inherent in the everyday. What Europeans referred to as "the Great Spirit" in Mahican is none other than *Pach-ta-mau-WAS*, literally "the One who is prayed to."

Manitoga, Spirit Ground, is a fitting name for this beautiful woods. In his mind, Wright saw the people of New York City as alienated from their natural environment. He built Manitoga for them, to come and experience the beauties of nature in an idealized temperate deciduous forest. To reattach their spirits to the spirit of the natural ecosystem. To feel the essence and soul of the woods.

Manitoga is different from other nature centers. Rather than teaching through the use of exhibits and signs, the landscape itself is the teaching tool, with the path the guide. Each path has a theme, and leads the walker through a sensual and experiential education. Wright understood that nature study is not only an intellectual process but also an aesthetic one.

The jewel in the lotus of Wright's forest is Dragon Rock, his house.

Built on the edge of the old quarry in what is now a waterfall and turquoise pool, Dragon Rock is one of the finest examples in the nation of building *with* the landscape.

The most recent educational addition to the grounds is one of the finest Native American encampments in the country, complete with a full-size, phragmites-insulated, tulip-bark wigwam, a flint-knapping or stone-tool-making area, drying and smoking racks, fire pits, skin stretching racks, stone mortars, and wooden troughs. At this site are

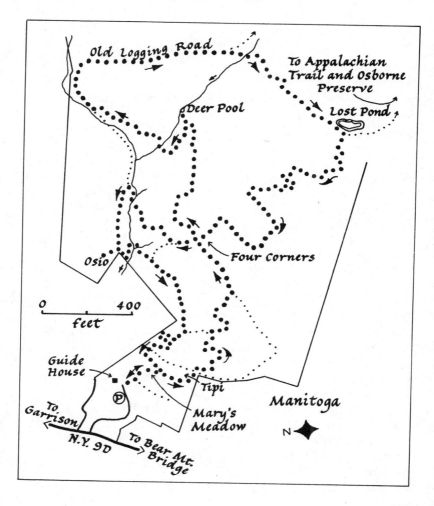

offered educational programs and hands-on workshops for schools and for the public.

ACCESS

Manitoga is located on the east side of NY 9D 2.5 miles north of the Bear Mountain Bridge. There is an entrance fee of $2 for adults, $1 for seniors and children. There is free admission every Tuesday. The grounds are open all year Monday through Friday, 9 AM to 4 PM; weekends from April to October, 10 AM to 6 PM. Dragon Rock and the Native American encampment are open by appointment only. No dogs are allowed. Phone: office, (914) 424-3812.

TRAIL

Rather than concerning ourselves with ecological facts, let's walk these trails as one would a garden. Opposite the office, the trail leads into Mary's Meadow, named for Wright's wife. Everything is placed here for aesthetic purposes: see how the bright open meadow contrasts against the dark shut-in hemlocks? Go through the meadow, to the right past the tipi. The trail enters the hemlocks. Take the left fork uphill on stone stairs—they are so unobtrusive, they seem perfectly natural. Pass mounds of velvet green moss and hemlocks grown against grey glacial boulders. The path is narrow and intimate. When the leaves are down, there are views through the deciduous trees of hills, Con Hook, and the Hudson River.

At the Four Corners, marked by a large hemlock in the center and log benches, go straight, toward the sound of falling water and uphill through the Fern Grove under oak and tulip trees. Visit the Deer Pool, at its best in spring when the stream curtains across a slab of bedrock. Pass the Fallen Giants, a hemlock and a white pine that fell in the 1976 hurricane, to a stand of white pines atop an outcrop ledge of bedrock. Turn right uphill. The trail is an old logging road from the mid-1800s. It leads to Lost Pond, a bowl quarried in the bedrock. The stone from Lost Pond was floated down the Hudson River and cemented into the foundation of the New York Public Library.

A trail to the left leads to the Appalachian Trail and Osborne Preserve; should you go this way, the path may at first be obscured and hard to pick up, but it soon becomes clear. Our tour of Manitoga continues by returning downhill to the Four Corners, keeping straight across to the stream. Turn left downstream. At the private sign, turn right for a sidetrip to the Osio. "Do not make the usual crude mistake of a panoramic vista by cutting down everything in front of the viewer," wrote Russell Wright. Rather, make osios, windows through the forest, framed with large trees and having "many trees between the viewer and the vista to create more depth and a subtle, natural effect." This osio has largely filled in, but the glacial boulders are impressive.

Recross the stream on a bridge. The path leads past more glacial boulders to the Laurel Field. European gardeners find it amazing that a bush as showy as mountain laurel grows wild and *in profusion* in America. The shrub is a landscape designer's dream come true. Swedish botanist Peter Kalm fell in love with the mountain laurel he discovered on the banks of the Hudson in the 1700s. As a pupil of Carl von Linne, the father of modern systematic botany, he needed to give a scientific name to his discovery, so he named it for himself: *Kalmia latifolia*.

Manitoga's tulip tree bark wigwam and Native encampment are among the regions' finest; open by appointment only.

Mountain laurel is at its finest in late May and early June when its pink candy flower buds open into pink, white, and red extravaganzas. The ten pollen-bearing male anthers each are tucked into ten pillows at the back of the flower's corolla. Touch one with the tip of a blade of grass, and it springs up dusting pollen onto the grass tip. If the grass had been a bee, she would be gold with pollen. When she lights on the next laurel flower, some of the male pollen will fall upon the female stigma to fertilize the eggs that will grow into seeds. To further protect this precious pollen from depredation by unsolicited ground-walking and climbing insects, the outside of the flower and all the branches are sticky.

Evergreen mountain laurel leaves are poisonous to cattle and sheep, which has led to names like sheep laurel and lambkill (names commonly applied to *K. angustifolia*, a smaller laurel of boggier ground). Peter Kalm described how if dogs happen to eat the entrails of a dead deer that had ingested mountain laurel leaves, they "become quite stupid, and, as it were, intoxicated, and often fall so sick that they seem to be at the point of death; but the people who have eaten the venison have not felt the least inconvenience." A volunteer fireman in Dutchess County told of a brushfire on the Harlem Valley's East Mountain that burned so hot he was struck unconscious by toxic fumes released from flaming mountain laurel. Dried mountain laurel wood, hard and fine-grained, can be carved into unparalleled forks, ladles, and spoons, which led to its other name of spoonwood. The wood was also used for the handles of small tools and for cogwheels.

Continue on the trail and you will find yourself back at Mary's Meadow.

37. Anthony's Nose

Location: Bear Mountain Bridge
Distance: 2.5 miles; 2 to 3 hours
Owner: Camp Smith, New York National Guard

Anthony's Nose straddles the Putnam–Westchester county border. Though short, the climb to the top is very steep, so give yourself a couple hours to complete your walk. From the summit, one views the entire stretch of the Hudson Highlands. During the autumn, Anthony's Nose is one of the best lookouts along the Hudson flyway for migrating hawks.

A mountain named for someone's schnozzle has given rise to all sorts of nonsense as to the origin of the name Anthony's Nose. The

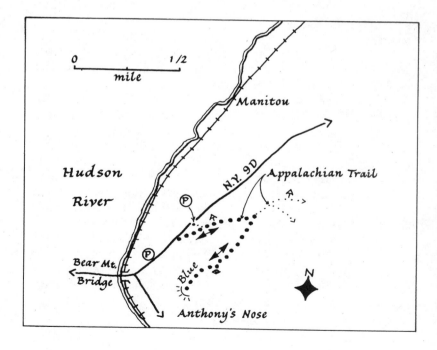

mountain was already so named in the 1697 deed that described the north boundary of Van Cortlandt Manor. Washington Irving wrote how the sun shone off the great nose of Peter Stuyvesant's trumpeter, Anthony von Corlear, and shot "hissing hot" into the water where it killed a sturgeon sporting beside Anthony's vessel. Well, we expect such stuff from Irving, but others go on to insist Anthony's Nose is named for St. Anthony, or for an old Hudson River Dutch captain with a mighty honker. Lossing just says that "the true origin of the name of this promontory is unknown." Let's leave it at that.

ACCESS

Park in pull-offs along NY 9D just north of the Bear Mountain Bridge. One pull-off is on the west side of NY 9D south of the trailhead. A bit further south, another smaller pull-off is on the east side of NY 9D just north of the trailhead.

TRAIL

You might want to start by walking out on the Bear Mountain Bridge for the view. Use the walkers' ramp. Sugarloaf stands upriver and all the Highlands spread out to the North Gate and South Beacon. Downriver is Peekskill Bay and the South Gate. Opposite is Popolopen Gorge, Bear Mountain, and Iona Island. And behind rises the steep rock face of 900-foot high Anthony's Nose.

From the bridge, walk north on NY 9D to the road sign for the Appalachian Trail, where the white blazes begin on the right, up stone stairs. Climb steeply, angling north through xeric chestnut oak and mountain laurel. After climbing into hemlocks, you will meet the wide old military road marked in blue blazes. Turn right. The walk from here is nearly level. Pass a woodland pool, and you are soon at the summit.

The Hudson River bends around Anthony's Nose in a triangular-faceted way. Before the Pleistocene, the river ran on the west side of Iona Island. See the old channel, where the Timp Brook curls through Salisbury Meadow? Originally, Anthony's Nose was a wider mountain. Iona Island was the foot of its slope. But there was a notch on the slope of Anthony's Nose. The most recent glacier severely eroded this notch and sheared off the foot of the mountain. Into this new channel the Hudson flowed, past an Anthony's Nose with a new look: triangular, known as a truncated spur.

Upriver, the glacier gouged out the sides and bottom of the Hudson, creating a deep gorge 1,000 feet below sea level at Storm King. The Bear Mountain Inn sits on a terrace that was the bed of the ancient Hudson River when it flowed in its old channel. Glaciation hollowed out the terrace where Hessian Lake now glints in the sun.

When the glaciers melted, the sea level rose, flooding the Hudson gorge and creating a true fjord. The only other fjord in the eastern United States is Somes Sound outside Acadia National Park in Maine.

Between Bear Mountain and Anthony's Nose, the Hudson River is up to 165 feet deep and is almost its narrowest: three-eighths of a mile wide. This is the deep and swift tidal Devil's Horse Race, or Horse Race, or simply the Race, the fastest and most dangerous section of the river for sail navigation, also known to skippers as the Crescent or Cook's Reach because of its crescent curve around Anthony's Nose.

The wind on top is strong as we survey a panorama that includes New York City, Haverstraw and Peekskill Bays, clear up the entire range of the Highlands. There is Manitou, a tiny village squeezed between the river and the railroad. Look what a huge mountain Bear Mountain is. Directly opposite, just north of Bear Mountain Bridge, is Popolopen Gorge.

In 1777, on the south side of Popolopen Gorge, stood Fort Clinton. On the north side stood Fort Montgomery. On top of Anthony's Nose was kept a signal beacon. Generals George and James Clinton, brothers, commanded the garrisons. The first Great Chain was a boom of floating logs and iron links, impenetrable, surely. It stretched from Fort Montgomery to Anthony's Nose. Two American frigates, the *Congress* and the *Montgomery*, rode at anchor above the chain. With two forts, two brothers, two frigates, and a Great Chain, let the British just try to get through!

Sir Henry Clinton, second-in-command of His Majesty's troops in New York (no relation to the brothers Clinton, nor had he yet earned the title "Sir"), wanted the Hudson River. He knew, and George Washington knew, that with this key valley the British could split the American colonies in two, and finish them off. Whoever controlled the Hudson River controlled America, and the revolution. Sir Henry Clinton sailed with his fleet from British-held New York City. He landed 2,000 men near Peek's Kill in a feint on General Israel Putnam's Fort Independence on the south slope of Anthony's Nose. The fog came in. Under cover, Clinton crossed the Hudson and landed 2,000 more men just south of Dunderberg. They split into two groups, one

The view from on top of Anthony's Nose downriver to the South Gate of the Highlands.

for each brother's fort. One group crept over Dunderberg as the other snuck through Timp Pass. At Lake Sinnipink, one group met Fort Clinton's picket guard and a detachment of rebels. The fight was bloody. When it was done, the British had won. They threw the bodies into the waters of Lake Sinnipink, so many bodies that the lake turned red with blood. Since then it's been called both Bloody Pond and Hessian Lake.

Sir Henry Clinton's Hessians continued towards Forts Clinton and Montgomery. By now, the Clinton brothers knew they were in for it. They were outnumbered, and their forts, vulnerable from the rear, fell to the British. The brothers escaped. George Clinton slid on the seat of his pants down the steep slope from the fort to a boat on the river. James, bayoneted in the thigh, escaped into the hills. On the river, the British fleet forced the Great Chain with ease. The two rebel frigates stationed just above, along with two galleys and an armed sloop, gave battle until the loss of the forts, then they turned upriver to flee. But the wind blew south. There was no escape. To keep the ships from British hands, the rebels set them afire, and the rebels jumped into the river.

Triumphant, Henry Clinton sailed up the Hudson. He planned to sail clear to Albany, where he would meet General Burgoyne coming south from Canada and, together, they would secure the Hudson corridor and the north. But, frustratingly, Clinton was recalled to New York City. He sent his man o'war under one of his officers to do the job. They sailed upriver, burning and looting to Poughkeepsie, then on to the state capital at Kingston where they burned "that nest of rebels" to the ground, and then to Clermont, likewise burning it to the ground. But they took too long. Burgoyne surrendered at the Battle of Saratoga, and the man o'war had nothing to do but return to New York City. The Hudson River, the key to the colonies and to the war, was left to the rebels.

On top of Anthony's Nose you can see all these places: Dunderberg, the distinctive hump of The Timp, the notch of Timp Pass, Hessian Lake, and the sites of the forts on either side of Popolopen Gorge.

In autumn, stand at the top of Anthony's Nose to watch the hawks. Down the ancient flypath of the Hudson Valley they zoom. The broad-winged hawks travel in large flocks that soar in a tight boiling pattern. Single falcons and accipiters shoot overhead. Bald eagles winter at Iona Island where the Hudson remains ice-free and they can continue to hunt for fish.

Iona Island, once a resort and then a military camp, now is one of four sites of the Hudson River National Estuarine Research Reserve. The other three are: Tivoli Bays, Piermont Marsh, and Stockport Flats. At Iona Island the sea breeze stops. This is as far inland as the mediating influence of the Atlantic Ocean reaches and is the dividing line between north and south ecosystems. South of Iona Island, the annual mean temperature is higher. Only fourteen miles north of Iona at Newburgh, spring comes two weeks later. South of Iona grow southern arrowwood and oblong fruited pinweed. North grows striped maple.

Off the military road are sidetrails that lead to glacier-smoothed bedrock outcrops with wider views south. Past the fire tower foundation is a wide view north. Return the same way you came.

Wilderstein, in Rhinebeck, Dutchess County.

Other Parks to Walk and Ramble Through

DUTCHESS COUNTY

Rudd Pond

Rudd Pond is one of the parcels of the Taconic State Park, located north of Millerton on Dutchess County 62/Rudd Pond road. Phone: office, (518) 789-3059. No dogs are allowed. Hours: 8 AM to 9 PM. A four-mile loop leads from the parking lot past the camping area to Manning's Ore Pit that is now a pond inhabited by beaver, then uphill alongside a stream where nest Louisiana waterthrush, through deciduous forest. Just before a brook, there is an obscure left turn that leads back downhill to an obscured end at the park's paved entrance road. You can walk along a power line right-of-way through a white pine plantation rather than along the road to return to your car. Numerous waterfowl stop at Rudd Pond in November. There are plans to link Rudd Pond with Brace Mountain via a ridge crest trail or via the Harlem Valley Rail Trail.

Harlem Valley Rail Trail

Purchased in 1989 and owned by New York State, the old Harlem Valley Railroad bed is being converted into a trail. From Wassaic, the rail trail runs for about twenty-three miles through the Harlem Valley north past extensive wetlands to Copake Falls in Columbia County. There are plans to eventually extend it to Chatham. Phone: Dutchess County Parks office at Bowdoin Park, (914) 297-1224.

Wilcox Park

Owned by Dutchess County, the 600-acre Wilcox Park, off NY 199 in Milan, would have had a chapter of its own in this book except for the Snowleaf Storm of 1987, which caused such a catastrophic windfall of trees that Wilcox's trails will take years to clear, if ever. Budget restrictions prevent trail maintenance. However, there are several paved and one dirt road through the wooded hills, plus many fields and streams to wander, picnic areas, and swimming and boating ponds. There is a $3 admission fee for parking. Dogs are allowed on leash only. The park is open between Memorial and Labor days, from

10 AM to 4 PM. Phone: office, (914) 758-6100, or Dutchess County Parks office at Bowdoin Park, (914) 297-1224.

Wilderstein

Thomas Holy Suckley built Wilderstein in a unique Queen Anne style in 1852 between the Hudson River and Morton Road in Rhinebeck. Wilderstein Preservation, Inc. opens the house on certain weekends in the summer. The woodland grounds were designed by Calvert Vaux and show views of the Hudson River past Hoyt House as far south as the Beacons. Phone: Wilderstein president Ray Armater, (914) 889-8344.

Edward R. Murrow Memorial Park

This eighty-six-acre municipal park off Old Route 55 and Lakeside Drive is leased by the Town of Pawling. Several short loop trails lead through successional fields and forest. On one hill stands the Burr Tree, an ancient sycamore. Just west on Old Route 55 are the extensive stone foundations of historic Coles Mills. Phone: Town of Pawling recreation office, (914) 855-1131.

Dennings Point

Acquired by New York State in 1989, Dennings Point juts out into the Hudson River's Newburgh Bay at the estuary mouth of Fishkill Creek in Beacon. Keep an eye out for the opening of this park; it is a jewel. If I could choose one place in Dutchess or Putnam to live, it might well be here. The sand island is flat and tillable, a site of varied uses from the early Native Americans to modern times. The eighty-acre bay of the Fishkill Creek mouth and the estuary stream itself up to the first waterfall in Beacon are irreplaceable spawning areas for anadromous fishes, the same as with Wappinger Creek as described in the Reese Sanctuary chapter. Osprey are especially prevalent. The views from Dennings Point are tremendous. Overhead looms the Beacon Range, to the north is Danskammer Point, west is Newburgh, and—best of all—south stands the imposing North Gate of the Hudson Highlands.

Innisfree Garden

Located on Tyrrell Road in Millbrook, this is one of the finest Chinese stroll gardens in the West. A cup garden, Walter Beck's Innisfree contains plants from all over the world, including groves of our own native species, some common, many rare. But Innisfree is not an

210

arboretum. Species are placed to celebrate the beauty of nature by creating a three-dimensional landscape painting around Tyrrell Lake.

The grounds are open May through October. Hours: Saturday and Sunday from 11 AM to 5 PM, when admission is charged ($2.00 per person sixteen years and older). Wednesday through Friday hours are 10 AM to 4 PM, and admission is free. Innisfree is also open on those Mondays that are legal holidays. No dogs are allowed. Phone: the director's home, (914) 677-8000.

PUTNAM COUNTY

Constitution Island

The British fleet fortified this strategic site, and named it after the body of laws and traditions that make up their country's constitution, but it was the Americans who took it over, refortified it extensively, stretched the second Great Chain across World's End, only to abandon Constitution Island for the higher ground of West Point. Owned by the U.S. Army, this island is used by West Point cadets for picnicking, but is open to the public on a very limited basis, as follows.

The Constitution Island Association runs guided tours from mid-June to October, Wednesday and Thursday afternoons, leaving West Point's South Dock at 1 and 2 PM. The one and one-half hour tour visits the Warner House, where you meet Susan and Anna Warner of the 1800s in a house built during the Revolutionary War, with later additions in the 1800s. Next, Yankee Doodle, a Revolutionary War soldier, leads you into the forest of red and black oak, white pine, and prickly pear to a few of the closer redoubt and battery foundations. Throughout the boat ride and walking tour are great views of World's End, Castle Rock, Sugarloaf Mountain, Canada Hill, Anthony's Nose, Crows Nest, Bull Hill, Breakneck, and Storm King. In other words, you are in the heart of the Hudson Highlands. From South Dock alone, one has a view from North to South Gate. Reservations are required. Call: Constitution Island Association, (914) 446-8676.

Appalachian Trail

As if Dutchess and Putnam counties were not already rich enough in history and walking trails, we also have the internationally famous Appalachian Trail. Conceived in 1921 by forester Benton MacKaye, the AT stretches for 2,135 miles—maintained solely by volunteers—from Maine to Georgia along the crest of the older Appalachians.

Thirty-two miles of the AT run through Dutchess County, twenty-four miles through Putnam. It is one of the longest marked footpaths in the world.

The trail enters Dutchess from the Schaghticoke Indian Reservation in Kent, Connecticut (the Schaghticoke are descendants of New England and Mahican Indians, given their reservation in the 1700s), meanders back across the state border, re-enters at Duell Hollow to traverse southwesterly to the Bear Mountain Bridge. Along the way, it encounters several of the parks covered in this book. Since there are shelters along the way, one could take a week-long backpacking trip.

The AT is well-documented by many publications. The New York–New Jersey Trail Conference publishes the detailed *Guide to the Appalachian Trail in New York and New Jersey*, complete with trail descriptions and topographic maps, available in bookstores.

Selected Bibliography

Adams, Arthur. *A Guidebook to the River.* State University of New York Press, Albany, N.Y. 1981.

Appalachian Mountain Club. *In the Hudson Highlands.* Walking News, Inc., New York, 1945.

Beers, F. W. *Atlas of New York and Vicinity.* Beers, Ellis and Soule, New York, 1867. Available at historical societies. This book covers the entire Hudson River shorelines and has a map for each town.

Boyle, Robert H. *The Hudson River, A Natural and Unnatural History.* W. W. Norton, New York; expanded ed., 1979.

Bruce, Wallace. *The Hudson.* Walking News, Inc., New York, 1982. Centennial edition.

Carmer, Carl. *The Hudson.* Holt, Rhinehart and Winston, New York, 1939. The Rivers of America Series.

Cronon, William. *Changes in the Land: Indians, Colonists, and the Ecology of New England.* Hill and Wang/Farrar, Straus and Giroux, New York, 1983.

Gekle, William F. *A Hudson Riverbook.* Wyvern House, Hamilton Reproductions, Poughkeepsie, N.Y., 1978.

Glunt, Ruth R. *Lighthouses and Legends of the Hudson.* Library Research Associates, Monroe, N.Y., 1975.

Howell, William Thompson. *The Hudson Highlands.* Walking News, Inc., New York, 1982.

Jameson, J. Franklin. *Narratives of New Netherland, Original Narratives of Early American History, 1609–1664.* Barnes and Nobel, Inc., New York, 1967.

Lossing, Benson. *The Hudson, From the Wilderness to the Sea.* New Hampshire Publishing Co., Somersworth, N.H., 1972. Facsimile of the 1866 edition.

McMartin, Barbara and Peter Kick. *Fifty Hikes in the Hudson Valley.* Backcountry Publications, Woodstock, Vt., 1985 (updated 1990).

New York–New Jersey Trail Conference. *New York Walk Book.* Anchor Books/Doubleday, New York; 5th ed., 1984.

O'Brien, Raymond J. *American Sublime, Landscape and Scenery of the Lower Hudson Valley.* Columbia University Press, New York, 1981.

Van Zandt, Roland. *Chronicles of the Hudson, Three Centuries of Travelers' Accounts.* Rutgers University Press, New Brunswick, N.J., 1971.

Wyckoff, Jerome. *Rock Scenery of the Hudson Highlands and Palisades.* Adirondack Mountain Club, Glens Falls, N.Y., 1971.

Index

More from The Countryman Press and Backcountry Publications

New England Guides from our Walks & Rambles Series
Walks & Rambles on Cape Cod & the Islands
Walks & Rambles in Rhode Island
More Walks & Rambles in Rhode Island
Walks & Rambles in the Upper Connecticut River Valley

Explorer's Guides
Cape Cod & the Islands: An Explorer's Guide
Connecticut: An Explorer's Guide
The Hudson Valley & Catskill Mountains: An Explorer's Guide
Maine: An Explorer's Guide
New Hampshire: An Explorer's Guide
Rhode Island: An Explorer's Guide
Vermont: An Explorer's Guide

New England Guides from our Hiking Series
Fifty Hikes in Connecticut
Fifty Hikes in Massachusetts
Fifty Hikes in Northern Maine
Fifty Hikes in Southern Maine
Fifty Hikes in Vermont
Fifty Hikes in the White Mountains
Fifty More Hikes in New Hampshire

Also
New England's Special Places
Canoeing Massachusetts, Rhode Island, & Massachusetts
Canoe Camping Vermont & New Hampshire Rivers

Our books are available through bookstores, or they may be ordered directly from the publisher. VISA/Mastercard accepted. For ordering information or for a complete catalog, please contact:

The Countryman Press
P.O. Box 175AP
Woodstock, VT 05091-0175
or call our toll-free number: (800) 245-4151